Early Childhood Activities for Creative Educators

Early Childhood Activities for Creative Educators

PAMELA S. BRIGGS
MCLENNAN COMMUNITY COLLEGE

THEO L. PILOT
EARLY CHILDHOOD CONSULTANT

JANET H. BAGBY
BAYLOR UNIVERSITY

Africa • Australia • Canada • Denmark • Japan • Mexico • New Zealand • Philippines
Puerto Rico • Singapore • Spain • United Kingdom • United States

NOTICE TO THE READER

Delmar Staff:

Business Unit Director: Susan L. Simpfenderfer
Executive Editor: Marlene McHugh Pratt
Acquisitions Editor: Erin O'Connor Traylor
Executive Production Manager: Wendy A. Troeger

Production Editor: Sandra Woods
Technology Project Manager: Kimberly Schryer
Executive Marketing Manager: Donna J. Lewis
Channel Manager: Nigar Hale
Editorial Assistant: Alexis Ferraro

Cover Design: Linda Demasi

For more information, contact Delmar, 3 Columbia Circle, PO Box 15015, Albany, NY 12212-0515; or find us on the World Wide Web at http://www.delmar.com or http://www.EarlyChildEd.Delmar.com

International Division List

Asia:
Thomson Learning
60 Albert Street, #15-01
Albert Complex
Singapore 189969

Thomas Nelson & Sons LTD
Nelson House
Mayfield Road
Walton-on-Thames
KT 12 5PL United Kingdom

Canada:
Nelson/Thomson Learning
1120 Birchmount Road
Scarborough, Ontario
Canada M1K 5G4

Japan:
Thomson Learning
Palaceside Building 5F
1-1-1 Hitotsubashi, Chiyoda-ku
Tokyo 100 0003 Japan

Latin America:
Thomson Learning
Seneca, 53
Colonia Polanco
11560 Mexico D.F. Mexico

Spain:
Thomson Learning
Calle Magallanes, 25
28015-MADRID
ESPANA

Australia/New Zealand:
Nelson/Thomson Learning
102 Dodds Street
South Melbourne, Victoria 3205
Australia

South Africa:
Thomson Learning
Zonnebloem Building
Constantia Square
526 Sixteenth Road
P.O. Box 2459
Halfway House, 1685
South Africa

International Headquarters:
Thomson Learning
International Division
290 Harbor Drive, 2nd Floor
Stamford, CT 06902-7477

UK/Europe/Middle East:
Thomson Learning
Berkshire House
168-173 High Holborn
London
WC1V 7AA United Kingdom

Library of Congress Cataloging-in-Publication Data

Briggs, Pamela S.
    Early childhood activities for creative educators / Pamela Briggs, Theo Pilot, Janet Bagby.
p. cm.
    ISBN 0-7668-1610-9
1. Early childhood education—Activity programs. I. Pilot, Theo. II. Bagby, Janet. III. Title.

LB1139.35.A37 B75 2001
372.13—dc21

00-031636

Contents

Preface

Thank you for selecting *Early Childhood Activities for Creative Educators,* a resource book of unique learning activities. It was developed by three creative early childhood educators who have many years of experience working with young children. This book was published in response to requests from people who learned of these activity materials in workshops conducted by the authors.

This is a book that provides ideas and information for making learning activities for children. Children use the activities after the adult makes them. Children do not make the items described in the book.

Using this resource book, you can prepare activities from inexpensive and easily acquired items. Made as directed, these activities are of high quality and as durable as any activities used regularly by children. All of the activities have been proven to provide successful learning activities for young children.

This book includes something for everyone — from a new or inexperienced teacher or parent to an individual who has much experience and is looking for new ways to provide quality inexpensive learning activities for young children.

Step-by-step instructions are provided for adults to prepare the learning activities. The directions for each include: activity title, developmental levels of child, areas of development (physical, cognitive, social, and emotional), benefits to child, materials needed, and assembling information.

Directions are detailed and may appear simplistic. Our goal is to include a wide variety from which persons may choose to meet their own abilities to construct the learning activities. This book is organized by developmental age levels, which seems a logical method for adult selection of activity materials that are appropriate for children in their care. Some ideas about the environment and developmental norms that may be helpful in choosing activities are included in this preface.

Gathering and assembling activity materials may vary from the simple (i.e., POT SCRUBBERS) for two-year-olds, to more detailed and complex (i.e., SEW A NUMBER) for four- through seven-year-olds. Therefore, teachers, parents, and others who use the book, collect, and make the activity materials will make selections based on the developmental levels of children, their own creative skills and abilities, as well as the availability of the inexpensive and/or easily acquired items described.

Safety for young children is of foremost importance. To assure meeting developmental needs and safe use, the activities must be carefully selected by adults. The safety of materials and their use is the responsibility of the adult in charge. Early childhood teachers and parents are the individuals who can best select the most appropriate activities for the children in their care.

Developmental norms are helpful for teacher and parent in evaluating a child's development. Information is of value as adults provide experiences to support and enhance development at each child's stage of development. The developmental ages mentioned in this book are approximate for suggested use of the activities. Children with special needs, since they are more like other children than unlike, will benefit from the use of many of the activities.

All of the activities emphasize hands-on, active learning. Benefits for the child are listed, but each child who learns from the activities may also benefit in many other ways. The list is certainly not all-inclusive. Adults who prepare the activities must use judgment in determining age-appropriateness and safety of all materials and activities. Parents, who have young children at home, can both utilize the activities and learn about the benefits of the learning materials that can be prepared for their children. The activities included in this book were developed for hands-on learning and based on child development knowledge.

It is understood that there is a sequence in the growth and development of a child. Knowing where a child is in this sequence gives adults the information needed for planning for optimum development. As children use the materials and participate in activities, they learn about the connection between language, writing, and reading. They also learn mathematics using concrete objects included in the activities.

The child learns to write through many years of development, both physical and intellectual, and a wide variety of experiences. Writing and reading are closely related and adults should assist the child in learning the two together. The young child needs many opportunities to practice during this development. This book contains activities and information for a variety of stages in the development of the prewriting and writing skills.

Some milestones related to prewriting are:

- Up to one year a baby bangs and scribbles.
- By one and one-half years, the child scribbles.
- By three years, the child usually makes marks that may look like letters.
- At three and one-half years, the child may print a few large single letters—scattered anywhere on the page.
- At four years, printing is usually large and irregular—mostly beginning capitals (uppercase) of the child's first name.
- By five years, names are usually printed—often unevenly and with reverse letters.
- By six years, the child may print large letters, copy words, and often still reverses some letters.

The learning environment should be rich to encourage children to see the importance of words as they are learning about writing. As adults model and use spoken and printed words, the children quickly understand writing and its use in their everyday world.

Materials need to be provided in quantities depending on the developmental levels of children who will be using them. Listed below are many items that are appropriate for young children to use as they are learning to write. Items should be placed on low, open shelves for children to use. Specific writing experiences may be arranged by adults to meet the needs of an individual child or children in group settings.

PREWRITING MATERIALS

- puzzles
- clay
- zippers
- scissors
- easels
- fingerpaint
- magnetic board with magnetic shapes, numbers, and letters

- manipulatives
- sand
- buttons
- chalkboard and chalk
- hole punch
- blocks
- playdough
- paper for tearing and cutting

- hammers
- large stringing beads
- collage materials

WRITING CENTER MATERIALS

- pencils—large and small, various colors
- markers—nontoxic/ washable, large and small
- hold punch—various sizes
- dustless chalk—large and small
- rulers—all sizes
- index cards—unlined
- dictionary—age-appropriate
- magazines—for cutting activities

- paper—various sizes and shapes, newsprint, butcher paper on roll, construction paper, computer, typing, sandpaper
- calendars
- journals
- typewriter
- adding machine
- tracing paper
- colored circle stickers
- metal trays
- chalkboards
- staple puller

- word banks
- picture banks
- computer
- envelopes
- crayons—large and small, nontoxic
- magic slates
- glue—nontoxic
- lunch trays
- staplers

We are indebted to the many children and early childhood professionals who provided inspiration for this book. Special thanks to Kay Kocour and Bill Sobel for their assistance in completing *Early Childhood Activities for Creative Educators*. We hope you will find the activities helpful, and we welcome your suggestions and comments as you use this resource in teaching and caring for young children.

Reviewers

Audrey Beard
Albany State University
Albany, GA

Mary Kasindorf, Director
Child Care Center–KLASP
Glen Cove, NY

Debbie Simpson Smith, Ph.D.
San Jacinto College Central
Pasadena, TX

Jo-Ann Kosko Simmons
Greenville Central School
Greenville, NY

Dr. Violet Leathers
University of Akron
Silver Lake, OH

Susan L. Speroff
Northern Illinois University
DeKalb, IL

2 Years

Pot Scrubbers

DEVELOPMENTAL LEVEL: 2 Years

AREAS OF DEVELOPMENT: Cognitive, Physical, Social

BENEFITS TO CHILD: Eye-hand coordination; sensory experience—textures, sounds; sort by color; gross and fine motor development; cooperative play

MATERIALS:

- Clear plastic container with lid (4½" × 11")

- 6 plastic pot scrubbers (varied bright colors)

HOW TO MAKE:

✄ Place scrubbers in container.

Pot Scrubbers

STRATEGIES:

_____
_____
_____
_____
_____
_____
_____
_____

DEVELOPMENT:

_____
_____
_____
_____
_____
_____
_____
_____
_____
_____
_____

VARIATIONS:

_____
_____
_____
_____
_____
_____
_____
_____
_____
_____
_____
_____

Rings and Spools

DEVELOPMENTAL LEVEL: 2 Years

AREAS OF DEVELOPMENT: Cognitive, Physical, Social

BENEFITS TO CHILD: Eye-hand coordination; observe and separate colors; cooperative play; mathematics skills—counting rings

MATERIALS:

- 2 plastic thread spools (one ¾" diameter at top and 1⅝" diameter at bottom; one 1⅛" diameter at top and 1⅞" diameter at bottom)

- 12 plastic rings (2¾" diameter; varied colors)

- Plastic basket with handle to store materials

HOW TO MAKE:

- ✂ Store rings and spools in basket.

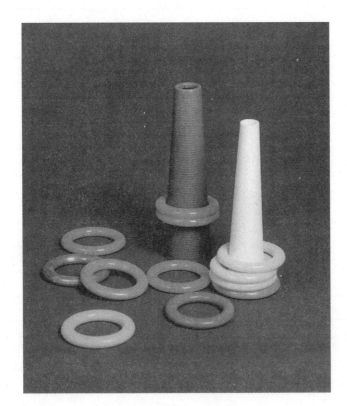

Rings and Spools

STRATEGIES:

_____
_____
_____
_____
_____
_____
_____
_____
_____

DEVELOPMENT:

_____
_____
_____
_____
_____
_____
_____
_____
_____
_____
_____

VARIATIONS:

_____
_____
_____
_____
_____
_____
_____
_____
_____
_____
_____
_____

Balls and Bells

DEVELOPMENTAL LEVEL: 2 Years

AREAS OF DEVELOPMENT: Cognitive, Physical, Social

BENEFITS TO CHILD: Gross motor development; sensory experience—sound, visual; roll with friend

MATERIALS:

- 3-gallon plastic water container
- Bell (1¼'')
- 3 colored Ping-Pong balls
- Hot glue gun and glue sticks

HOW TO MAKE:

- ✂ Place bell and balls in container.
- ✂ Attach top with hot glue.

Balls and Bells

STRATEGIES:

_____
_____
_____
_____
_____
_____
_____
_____
_____

DEVELOPMENT:

_____
_____
_____
_____
_____
_____
_____
_____
_____
_____
_____

VARIATIONS:

_____
_____
_____
_____
_____
_____
_____
_____
_____
_____
_____
_____

Ball Bottle

DEVELOPMENTAL LEVEL: 2 Years

AREAS OF DEVELOPMENT: Cognitive, Physical

BENEFITS TO CHILD: Sensory experience—visual, auditory; motor development; observes cause and effect

MATERIALS:

- Clear plastic container with lid (2-quart size)
- 6 Ping-Pong balls (1⅜" diameter, multicolored)
- Hot glue gun and glue sticks

HOW TO MAKE:

- Place Ping-Pong balls in container.
- Attach lid with hot glue.

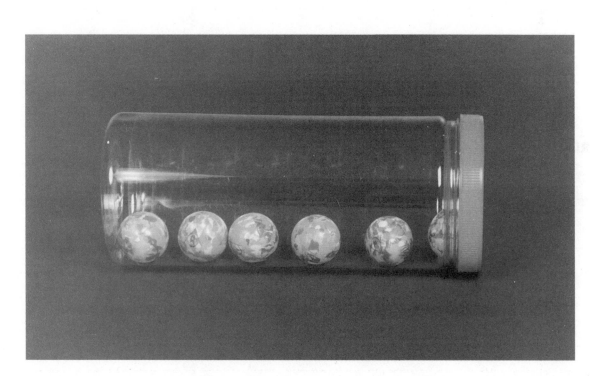

Ball Bottle

STRATEGIES:

_____
_____
_____
_____
_____
_____
_____
_____
_____

DEVELOPMENT:

_____
_____
_____
_____
_____
_____
_____
_____
_____
_____
_____

VARIATIONS:

_____
_____
_____
_____
_____
_____
_____
_____
_____
_____
_____
_____

Ball Tube

DEVELOPMENTAL LEVEL: 2 Years

AREAS OF DEVELOPMENT: Cognitive, Physical

BENEFITS TO CHILD: Sensory experience—sound, visual; physical development—gross and fine motor activities

MATERIALS:

- Plastic tube (24" × 1⅝" container that holds fluorescent light bulb replacements)
- 4 Ping-Pong balls (varied colors)
- Hot glue gun and glue sticks

HOW TO MAKE:

- Place balls in tube.
- Attach the two end pieces with hot glue.

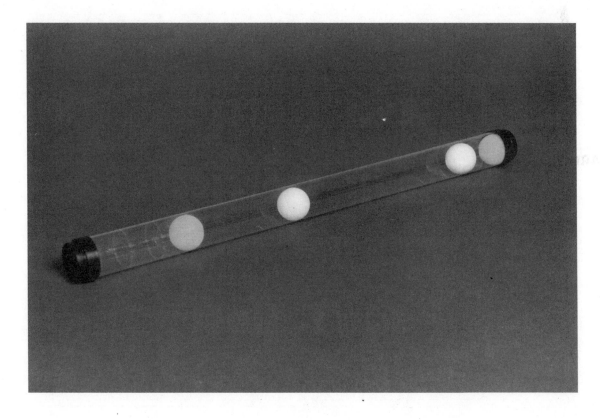

Ball Tube

STRATEGIES:

_____
_____
_____
_____
_____
_____
_____
_____

DEVELOPMENT:

_____
_____
_____
_____
_____
_____
_____
_____
_____
_____

VARIATIONS:

_____
_____
_____
_____
_____
_____
_____
_____
_____
_____
_____
_____

Toothbrush Holders

DEVELOPMENTAL LEVEL: 2 Years

AREAS OF DEVELOPMENT: Cognitive, Physical

BENEFITS TO CHILD: Fine and gross motor development; eye-hand coordination; sensory experience—sound, color, texture

MATERIALS:

- 3 toothbrush holders (bright colors)
- Heavy cord (3')

HOW TO MAKE:

- String toothbrush holders on cord.
- Tie knots in both ends of cord allowing approximately 8" of cord at one end.

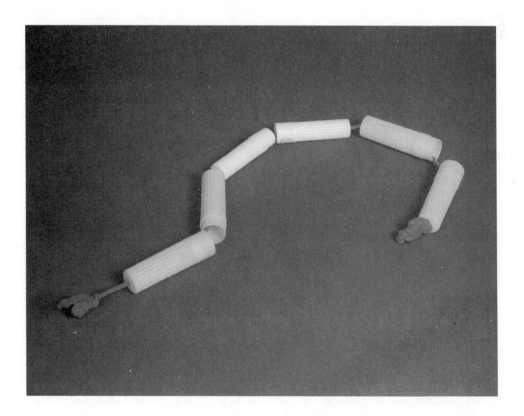

Toothbrush Holders

STRATEGIES:

_____
_____
_____
_____
_____
_____
_____
_____
_____

DEVELOPMENT:

_____
_____
_____
_____
_____
_____
_____
_____
_____
_____
_____

VARIATIONS:

_____
_____
_____
_____
_____
_____
_____
_____
_____
_____
_____
_____
_____

Texture Carry-Around

DEVELOPMENTAL LEVEL: 2 Years

AREAS OF DEVELOPMENT: Cognitive, Physical

BENEFITS TO CHILD: Fine and gross motor development; eye-hand coordination; sensory experience

MATERIALS:

- 2½-gallon plastic container
- Variety of textures in a variety of shapes for outside of container (4-inch square sandpaper, 6" × 6" Styrofoam red heart; 2" × 7" textured vinyl; 3" cardboard circle; three 1½" squares of carpet pieces in different colors; 1½" × 4" × ⅞" foam rubber; 2" × 7" green felt).
- Variety of items of various sizes, colors, and textures to carry (fifteen 3½" circles—plastic, felt, foam rubber, cardboard, plastic pot scrubber; 4" × 2 ½" × ⅞" foam rubber; scraps of fabrics—burlap, flannel, satin, fake fur, vinyl, and so forth.
- Hot glue gun and glue sticks
- Duct tape

Texture Carry-Around

HOW TO MAKE:

- ✂ Cut 3" × 5" opening around spout.
- ✂ Bind opening with duct tape.
- ✂ Attach textures and shapes to outside with hot glue.
- ✂ Place "to carry" items in container.

STRATEGIES:

_____

_____

_____

_____

_____

_____

_____

_____

_____

DEVELOPMENT:

_____

_____

_____

_____

_____

_____

_____

_____

_____

VARIATIONS:

_____

_____

_____

_____

_____

_____

_____

_____

_____

Nesting Bowls

DEVELOPMENTAL LEVELS: 2–3 Years

AREAS OF DEVELOPMENT: Cognitive, Physical

BENEFITS TO CHILD: Visual discrimination; matching; fine and gross motor development; eye-hand coordination; seriation

MATERIALS:

- 4 plastic mixing bowls (6", 7½", 9", and 10½")
- Set of lids to fit bowls (7⅜", 8¾", 10¼", and 11¾")

HOW TO MAKE:

- ✂ Purchase items listed.

Nesting Bowls

STRATEGIES:

_____

_____

_____

_____

_____

_____

_____

_____

_____

_____

_____

DEVELOPMENT:

_____

_____

_____

_____

_____

_____

_____

_____

_____

_____

VARIATIONS:

_____

_____

_____

_____

_____

_____

_____

_____

_____

_____

_____

_____

Bell Roller

DEVELOPMENTAL LEVELS: 2–3 Years

AREAS OF DEVELOPMENT: Cognitive, Physical

BENEFITS TO CHILD: Sensory experience—sound, visual; fine and gross motor development; mathematics concepts—number, counting

MATERIALS:

- Three 1'' bells
- Clear plastic mailing tube (12'' × 3'')
- Hot glue gun and glue sticks

HOW TO MAKE:

- Place bells in container.
- Attach end pieces to container with hot glue.

Bell Roller

STRATEGIES:

_____
_____
_____
_____
_____
_____
_____
_____

DEVELOPMENT:

_____
_____
_____
_____
_____
_____
_____
_____
_____

VARIATIONS:

_____
_____
_____
_____
_____
_____
_____
_____
_____
_____

Green Grass Roller

DEVELOPMENTAL LEVELS: 2–3 Years

AREAS OF DEVELOPMENT: Cognitive, Physical

BENEFITS TO CHILD: Sensory experience; fine motor development; language development

MATERIALS:

- Shiny "plastic grass" (½ package shredded glitter wrap)
- Plastic container with lid (11" × 4")
- Hot glue gun and glue sticks

HOW TO MAKE:

- ✂ Place "grass" in container.
- ✂ Attach lid with hot glue.

Green Grass Roller

STRATEGIES:

_____
_____
_____
_____
_____
_____
_____
_____
_____

DEVELOPMENT:

_____
_____
_____
_____
_____
_____
_____
_____
_____
_____
_____

VARIATIONS:

_____
_____
_____
_____
_____
_____
_____
_____
_____
_____
_____
_____

Ducks and Fish

DEVELOPMENTAL LEVELS: 2–3 Years

AREAS OF DEVELOPMENT: Cognitive, Physical

BENEFITS TO CHILD: Sensory experience; language development; fine and gross motor development

MATERIALS:

- Fabric bolt (8" × 23")
- Colored self-adhesive plastic (18" × 28")
- Self-stick antislip decals (4 large and 4 small ducks and 3 fish)

HOW TO MAKE:

- Cover fabric bolt with colored plastic.
- Attach ducks on one side of fabric bolt and fish on the other side.

Ducks and Fish

STRATEGIES:

_____
_____
_____
_____
_____
_____
_____
_____
_____
_____

DEVELOPMENT:

_____
_____
_____
_____
_____
_____
_____
_____
_____
_____

VARIATIONS:

_____
_____
_____
_____
_____
_____
_____
_____
_____
_____
_____
_____

Put In—Take Out

DEVELOPMENTAL LEVELS: 2–3 Years

AREAS OF DEVELOPMENT: Cognitive, Physical, Social

BENEFITS TO CHILD: Sensory experience; eye-hand coordination; matching; cooperative play; language development

MATERIALS:

- 4 plastic containers (8½" high with 2½" openings)
- Solid color self-adhesive plastic or laminate (7½" × 44")
- Solid-colored pieces of fabric (four or five 10" × 18" pieces of each color—red, yellow, blue, orange)

- Scissors
- Disinfectant (¼ cup chlorine bleach in one gallon of water)

Put In—Take Out

HOW TO MAKE:

- ✂ Clean containers with disinfectant and air-dry.

- ✂ Cut self-adhesive plastic or laminate into 7½" × 11" pieces and cover the containers.

- ✂ Place fabric pieces in containers.

STRATEGIES:

_____

_____

_____

_____

_____

_____

_____

DEVELOPMENT:

_____

_____

_____

_____

_____

_____

_____

_____

VARIATIONS:

_____

_____

_____

_____

_____

_____

_____

_____

_____

Pillow Textures

DEVELOPMENTAL LEVELS: 2–3 Years

AREAS OF DEVELOPMENT: Cognitive, Physical

BENEFITS TO CHILD: Sensory experience; language development

MATERIALS:

- 14" × 14" Pillow (use purchased pillow or make)
- Variety of 10" × 18" washable fabrics in a variety of textures such as taffeta, corduroy, fake fur, satin, and so forth.
- 14" zipper
- Sewing machine

Pillow Textures

HOW TO MAKE:

- ✂ Sew zipper between two pieces of fabric—on 10" sides.
- ✂ Sew the other two pieces of fabric together to form 18" square.
- ✂ With "right" sides together, sew around outside (all four sides of pillow cover).
- ✂ Unzip zipper and turn pillow cover with "right" side out.
- ✂ Topstitch all four sides ½" from edges.
- ✂ Place pillow inside pillow cover.

STRATEGIES:

_____
_____
_____
_____
_____
_____
_____

DEVELOPMENT:

_____
_____
_____
_____
_____
_____
_____
_____
_____

VARIATIONS:

_____
_____
_____
_____
_____
_____
_____
_____

Scatter the Balls

DEVELOPMENTAL LEVEL: 2–3 Years

AREAS OF DEVELOPMENT: Cognitive, Physical, Social

BENEFITS TO CHILD: Curiosity; fine and gross motor development; mathematics concepts; cooperative play

MATERIALS:

- Window tinting film holder with ends (20" × 3")
- 7 tennis balls in variety of colors

HOW TO MAKE:

- ✂ Store in box with balls inside tube.

Scatter the Balls

STRATEGIES:

_____
_____
_____
_____
_____
_____
_____
_____
_____
_____

DEVELOPMENT:

_____
_____
_____
_____
_____
_____
_____
_____
_____
_____
_____

VARIATIONS:

_____
_____
_____
_____
_____
_____
_____
_____
_____
_____
_____

Clothespin Clipping

DEVELOPMENTAL LEVELS: 2–4 Years

AREAS OF DEVELOPMENT: Cognitive, Physical, Social

BENEFITS TO CHILD: Eye-hand coordination; fine motor development; cooperative play; visual discrimination; sensory experience

MATERIALS:

- 100 large wooden clothespins
- Cardboard box (10½" × 14" × 4")
- Solid color self-adhesive plastic or laminate (18" × 40")
- Clear plastic gallon container
- Square 1–pint plastic storage container with lid with edge narrow enough on which to slip clothespins.

HOW TO MAKE:

- ✂ Cover cardboard box with self-adhesive plastic or laminate.
- ✂ Collect all materials.
- ✂ Cut 3½" from bottom of gallon container.

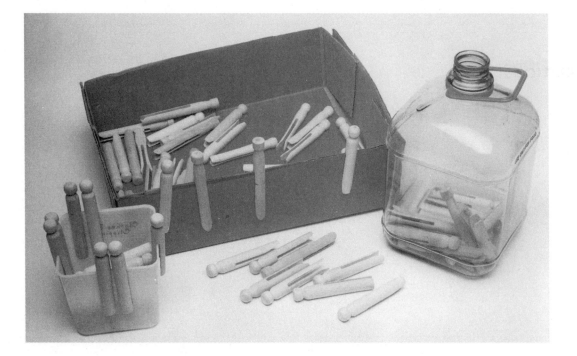

Clothespin Clipping

STRATEGIES:

_____
_____
_____
_____
_____
_____
_____
_____
_____
_____

DEVELOPMENT:

_____
_____
_____
_____
_____
_____
_____
_____
_____
_____
_____

VARIATIONS:

_____
_____
_____
_____
_____
_____
_____
_____
_____
_____
_____
_____

Hammering

DEVELOPMENTAL LEVELS: 2–4 Years

AREAS OF DEVELOPMENT: Cognitive, Physical

BENEFITS TO CHILD: Eye-hand coordination; fine motor development; cause and effect

MATERIALS:

- 5 fabric bolts
- Duct tape
- Plastic or wooden hammer
- Golf tees (4" tees, available at golf pro shops)
- Plastic container (with screw-on lid, e.g., peanut butter container)
- Hot glue gun and glue sticks
- Sticky back Velcro (2")

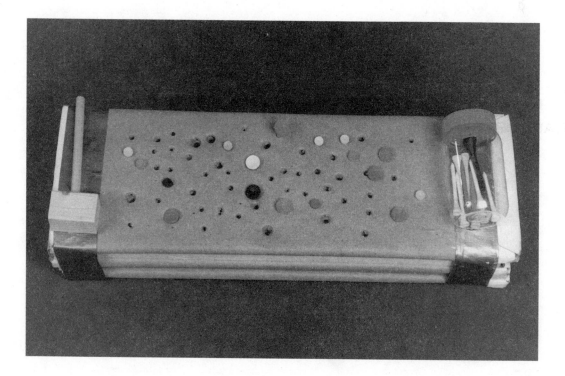

Hammering

HOW TO MAKE:

- ✄ Tape fabric bolts together securely with duct tape.

- ✄ Attach sticky back Velcro to hammer and the other side of the Velcro to fabric bolts (near one end).

- ✄ Hot glue plastic container near opposite end.

STRATEGIES:

_____
_____
_____
_____
_____
_____
_____
_____

DEVELOPMENT:

_____
_____
_____
_____
_____
_____
_____
_____

VARIATIONS:

_____
_____
_____
_____
_____
_____
_____
_____

Soft and Fuzzy

DEVELOPMENTAL LEVELS: 2–5 Years

AREAS OF DEVELOPMENT: Cognitive, Physical

BENEFITS TO CHILD: Creativity; sensory experience; language development

MATERIALS:

- Soft, fuzzy animal toys (from pet department)
- Car polishing mittens

HOW TO MAKE:

- Purchase items listed.

Soft and Fuzzy

STRATEGIES:

_____
_____
_____
_____
_____
_____
_____
_____

DEVELOPMENT:

_____
_____
_____
_____
_____
_____
_____
_____
_____
_____

VARIATIONS:

_____
_____
_____
_____
_____
_____
_____
_____
_____
_____
_____

Sound and Texture

DEVELOPMENTAL LEVELS: 2–5 Years

AREAS OF DEVELOPMENT: Cognitive, Physical

BENEFITS TO CHILD: Sensory experience; creativity; cause and effect; exploration

MATERIALS:

- Heavy corrugated cardboard (11" × 14")
- Duct tape
- 2 plastic canvases (11" × 14" each)
- Variety of paper and crayons

HOW TO MAKE:

- Place plastic canvas on both sides of cardboard.
- Place duct tape around the four edges holding the three layers together.

Sound and Texture

STRATEGIES:

_____
_____
_____
_____
_____
_____
_____
_____
_____

DEVELOPMENT:

_____
_____
_____
_____
_____
_____
_____
_____
_____
_____
_____

VARIATIONS:

_____
_____
_____
_____
_____
_____
_____
_____
_____
_____
_____

Watch Me Jar

DEVELOPMENTAL LEVELS: 2–5 Years

AREAS OF DEVELOPMENT: Cognitive, Physical

BENEFITS TO CHILD: Curiosity; cause and effect; observation skills; quiet play; sensory experience

MATERIALS:

- 1-gallon clear plastic container with lid (e.g., pickle, mayonnaise)
- 2 cups syrup
- 1 small package of sequins
- Hot glue gun and glue sticks
- Yellow food coloring

HOW TO MAKE:

- Place syrup, sequins, and 3 drops of food coloring in container.
- Attach lid to container with hot glue.

Watch Me Jar

STRATEGIES:

_____
_____
_____
_____
_____
_____
_____
_____
_____

DEVELOPMENT:

_____
_____
_____
_____
_____
_____
_____
_____
_____
_____

VARIATIONS:

_____
_____
_____
_____
_____
_____
_____
_____
_____
_____
_____
_____

All-in-One Chalkboard

DEVELOPMENTAL LEVELS: 2–5 Years

AREAS OF DEVELOPMENT: Cognitive, Physical

BENEFITS TO CHILD: Eye-hand coordination; creativity; sensory experience

MATERIALS:

- Clipboard (legal size)
- Chalkboard paint
- Paintbrush
- Sticky back Velcro (5")
- Chalk eraser
- Dustless chalk (¾" diameter)
- Cord (2')
- Hot glue gun and glue sticks

All-in-One Chalkboard

HOW TO MAKE:

✂ Paint clipboard on both sides with chalkboard paint (two coats).

✂ Attach one side of Velcro to eraser and the other side of Velcro to clip at top of clipboard.

✂ Put hot glue on chalk and tie on string and tie to hole at top of clipboard.

STRATEGIES:

_____
_____
_____
_____
_____
_____
_____
_____

DEVELOPMENT:

_____
_____
_____
_____
_____
_____
_____
_____

VARIATIONS:

_____
_____
_____
_____
_____
_____
_____
_____

Chalkboard

DEVELOPMENTAL LEVELS: 2–5 Years

AREAS OF DEVELOPMENT: Cognitive, Physical, Social

BENEFITS TO CHILD: Creativity; self-concept; eye-hand coordination; sensory experience

MATERIALS:

- Heavy corrugated cardboard (20" × 24")
- Chalkboard paint
- Paintbrush
- Duct tape
- Velcro (3")
- Dustless chalk (1" diameter)
- Cord (2')
- Chalkboard eraser

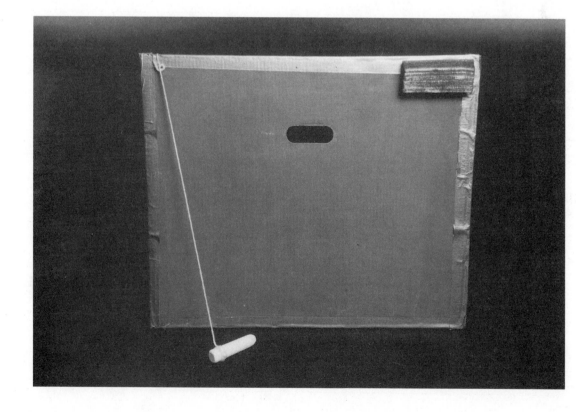

Chalkboard

HOW TO MAKE:

- ✂ Paint both sides of cardboard with 3 coats of paint and let dry.
- ✂ Place duct tape around all edges of chalkboard.
- ✂ Punch hole near upper left corner of chalkboard and tie on cord.
- ✂ Attach chalk securely to other end of cord.
- ✂ Cut Velcro into 1" pieces and attach one side of each piece to upper right corner of chalkboard and the other side of Velcro to eraser.
- ✂ Place eraser on chalkboard for storage.

STRATEGIES:

_____
_____
_____
_____
_____
_____
_____

DEVELOPMENT:

_____
_____
_____
_____
_____
_____
_____

VARIATIONS:

_____
_____
_____
_____
_____
_____
_____
_____

Drop by Drop

DEVELOPMENTAL LEVELS: 2–6 Years

AREAS OF DEVELOPMENT: Cognitive, Emotional, Social

BENEFITS TO CHILD: Creativity; fine motor development; eye-hand coordination; sensory experience; visual discrimination; self-concept development; cooperative play

MATERIALS:

- Plastic ice trays—an assortment including green, orange, blue and green
- Light blue small circle tray
- Red trays with 26 letters of alphabet
- 3 plastic medicine droppers
- 2 plastic liquid basters
- 2 clear plastic containers (1- to 2-cup capacity)
- Food coloring

Drop by Drop

✂ Collect materials.

STRATEGIES:

_____
_____
_____
_____
_____
_____
_____
_____
_____
_____

DEVELOPMENT:

_____
_____
_____
_____
_____
_____
_____
_____
_____
_____

VARIATIONS:

_____
_____
_____
_____
_____
_____
_____
_____
_____
_____
_____

Puppets

DEVELOPMENTAL LEVELS: 2–6 Years

AREAS OF DEVELOPMENT: Cognitive, Physical, Social

BENEFITS TO CHILD: Creativity; fine motor development; language development; eye-hand coordination; role-playing; vocabulary building; sequencing; cooperative play

MATERIALS:

- Hand and finger puppets
- Gloves for making puppets

HOW TO MAKE:

- ✂ Purchase or make a variety of hand and finger puppets—people, animals, story characters, and so forth.

Puppets

STRATEGIES:

_____
_____
_____
_____
_____
_____
_____
_____
_____

DEVELOPMENT:

_____
_____
_____
_____
_____
_____
_____
_____
_____
_____
_____

VARIATIONS:

_____
_____
_____
_____
_____
_____
_____
_____
_____
_____
_____
_____

Bag Writing

DEVELOPMENTAL LEVELS: 2–6 Years

AREAS OF DEVELOPMENT: Cognitive, Emotional, Physical, Social

BENEFITS TO CHILD: Creativity; sensory experience; concept development; eye-hand coordination; fine motor development; visual discrimination

MATERIALS:

- 2 clear plastic quilt bags with zipper closures (16" × 18")
- Container of shaving cream or 2 cups of finger paint for each bag (See recipe on Resource Information page in the Appendix.)

HOW TO MAKE:

- ✂ Make finger paint or purchase shaving cream.
- ✂ Put finger paint or shaving cream inside plastic bags.

Bag Writing

STRATEGIES:

_____
_____
_____
_____
_____
_____
_____
_____
_____

DEVELOPMENT:

_____
_____
_____
_____
_____
_____
_____
_____
_____
_____
_____

VARIATIONS:

_____
_____
_____
_____
_____
_____
_____
_____
_____
_____
_____

Glove Match

DEVELOPMENTAL LEVELS: 2–6 Years

AREAS OF DEVELOPMENT: Cognitive, Physical, Social

BENEFITS TO CHILD: Observation skills; organizational skills; words and concrete items; mathematics concepts—matching one-to-one correspondence

MATERIALS:

- 1-gallon plastic container (e.g., pickles, mayonnaise)
- 5 pairs of gloves (various colors and sizes)
- Card (3" × 5") for label
- Black permanent marker (wide point)
- Clear tape (2" × 12") for attaching label

HOW TO MAKE:

- Write "Glove Match" on label card.
- Attach label card to container with tape (cover completely).
- Place gloves in container.

Glove Match

STRATEGIES:

_____
_____
_____
_____
_____
_____
_____
_____
_____
_____

DEVELOPMENT:

_____
_____
_____
_____
_____
_____
_____
_____
_____
_____

VARIATIONS:

_____
_____
_____
_____
_____
_____
_____
_____
_____
_____
_____
_____

Color Windows

DEVELOPMENTAL LEVELS: 2–6 Years

AREAS OF DEVELOPMENT: Cognitive, Physical

BENEFITS TO CHILD: Sensory experience; compare and contrast; observation skills

MATERIALS:

- 2 pieces corrugated cardboard (10" × 17" each)
- 2 acetate report covers (7" × 8" each; one red and one blue)
- Duct tape
- Hot glue gun and glue sticks
- Utility knife

Color Windows

HOW TO MAKE:

- ✂ Cut 2 openings (5" × 7") in each piece of cardboard—one rectangle vertical and the other rectangle horizontal.

- ✂ Place acetate report covers in openings and attach to cardboard with tape.

- ✂ Attach duct tape to all sides of cardboard holding layers together securely.

STRATEGIES:

DEVELOPMENT:

VARIATIONS:

Color in Circles

DEVELOPMENTAL LEVELS: 2–6 Years

AREAS OF DEVELOPMENT: Cognitive, Physical

BENEFITS TO CHILD: Eye-hand coordination; fine motor development; cause and effect; color concepts; problem solving skills; observation skills

MATERIALS:

- 18" diameter Lazy Susan (or other available sizes)
- 15½" diameter circles of white paper (or sizes to fit available Lazy Susans)
- Nontoxic, washable markers in 12 colors
- Plastic tray (3¼" × 10")
- 4 cups plaster of paris
- Water for mixing plaster of paris
- Detergent lid for holding markers

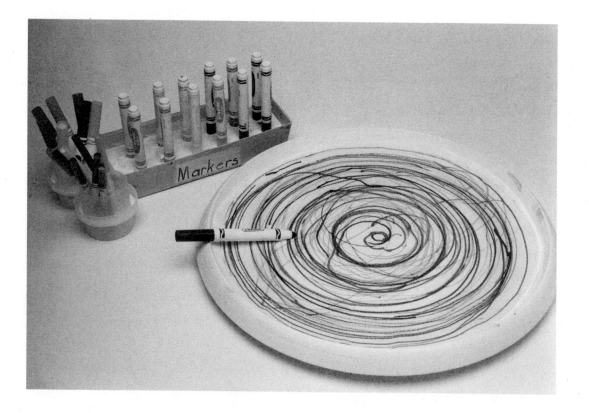

Color in Circles

HOW TO MAKE:

- Mix plaster of paris in tray.

- When plaster of paris thickens, place markers with tops down into plaster of paris.

- Write "Markers" on side of tray.

- Cut circles of paper and place on Lazy Susan.

STRATEGIES:

_____

_____

_____

_____

_____

_____

_____

DEVELOPMENT:

_____

_____

_____

_____

_____

_____

_____

_____

VARIATIONS:

_____

_____

_____

_____

_____

_____

_____

_____

_____

Story Apron

DEVELOPMENTAL LEVELS: 2–6 Years

AREAS OF DEVELOPMENT: Cognitive, Emotional, Physical, Social

BENEFITS TO CHILD: Language development; visual discrimination; matching; mathematics concept; creativity

MATERIALS:

- Apron (45" × 26")
- 9 fabric pockets (6" × 6") in primary and secondary colors
- 9" × 12" felt pieces (brown, yellow, red, green, blue, black, white) for items in stories such as *Goldilocks and the Three Bears* or *Gregory's Garden* or numbers one through nine
- 15 to 20 index cards (3" × 5")
- Clear self-adhesive plastic or laminate (18" × 24")
- ¾" squares of Velcro (for felt items)
- Sewing machine
- Scissors
- Permanent black marker

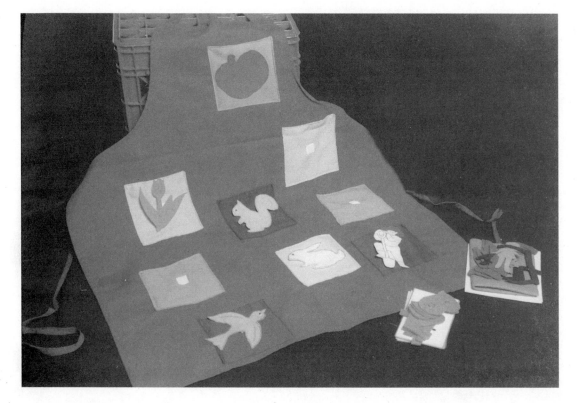

Story Apron

HOW TO MAKE:

- ✂ Make or purchase apron.
- ✂ Hem top edge of each pocket.
- ✂ Attach Velcro piece (loop side) to center of each pocket (sew if necessary to attach firmly).
- ✂ Make story items (using pictures from story or book) and numbers one through nine.
- ✂ Attach Velcro piece (hook side) to each story item and number.
- ✂ Write numbers one through nine on index cards with permanent black marker.
- ✂ Cover index cards (front and back) with self-adhesive plastic or laminate.

STRATEGIES:

_____
_____
_____
_____
_____
_____
_____

DEVELOPMENT:

_____
_____
_____
_____
_____
_____

VARIATIONS:

_____
_____
_____
_____
_____
_____
_____

Playdough

DEVELOPMENTAL LEVELS: 2–7 Years

AREAS OF DEVELOPMENT: Cognitive, Physical

BENEFITS TO CHILD: Fine motor development; eye-hand coordination; creativity; concept development; sensory experience

MATERIALS:

- Serving tray (12" × 16")
- Utensils, materials, and equipment for "making" playdough
- Playdough—purchased or made from recipe (See recipe on Resource Information page in the Appendix.)

HOW TO MAKE:

- ✂ Prepare homemade playdough.

Playdough

STRATEGIES:

_____
_____
_____
_____
_____
_____
_____
_____
_____

DEVELOPMENT:

_____
_____
_____
_____
_____
_____
_____
_____
_____
_____
_____

VARIATIONS:

_____
_____
_____
_____
_____
_____
_____
_____
_____
_____
_____
_____

Clippies

DEVELOPMENTAL LEVELS: 3–4 Years

AREAS OF DEVELOPMENT: Cognitive, Physical, Social

BENEFITS TO CHILD: Eye-hand coordination; color concepts; fine motor development; cooperative play

MATERIALS:

- Small bag of 2" clips (6 of each color—white, yellow, and red)
- Plastic or cardboard pencil box (8½" × 2½" × 5½")
- Solid color self-adhesive plastic (12" × 20")
- Scissors

HOW TO MAKE:

- Cover pencil box (if cardboard) with self-adhesive plastic.
- Place clips inside pencil box.

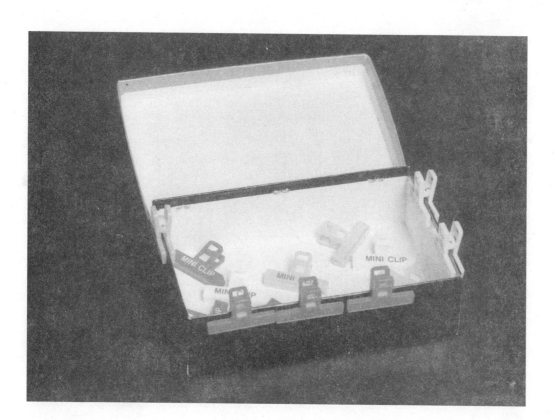

Clippies

STRATEGIES:

_____
_____
_____
_____
_____
_____
_____
_____
_____
_____

DEVELOPMENT:

_____
_____
_____
_____
_____
_____
_____
_____
_____
_____

VARIATIONS:

_____
_____
_____
_____
_____
_____
_____
_____
_____
_____
_____
_____

Duck Puzzle

DEVELOPMENTAL LEVELS: 3–4 Years

AREAS OF DEVELOPMENT: Cognitive, Physical

BENEFITS TO CHILD: Fine motor development; eye-hand coordination; problem solving; language development

MATERIALS:

- "Duck" plastic placemat (15" × 17")
- Red felt (16" × 19")
- Box for storage (9" × 11½")
- Colored self-adhesive plastic or laminate (16" × 20")

HOW TO MAKE:

- ✂ Purchase placemat.
- ✂ Cut placemat into 4 irregular pieces.
- ✂ Cover box top with self-adhesive plastic or laminate.
- ✂ Store felt and puzzle pieces in box.

Duck Puzzle

STRATEGIES:

_____
_____
_____
_____
_____
_____
_____
_____
_____
_____

DEVELOPMENT:

_____
_____
_____
_____
_____
_____
_____
_____
_____
_____

VARIATIONS:

_____
_____
_____
_____
_____
_____
_____
_____
_____
_____
_____
_____

Let's Lace

DEVELOPMENTAL LEVELS: 3–5 Years

AREAS OF DEVELOPMENT: Cognitive, Physical

BENEFITS TO CHILD: Creativity; eye-hand coordination; fine motor development; quiet play

MATERIALS:

- 4 plastic paint mixers (4½" × 8")
- 4 brightly colored shoestrings
- Fabric bag for storing

HOW TO MAKE:

- ✂ Tie a shoestring to handle of paint mixer.

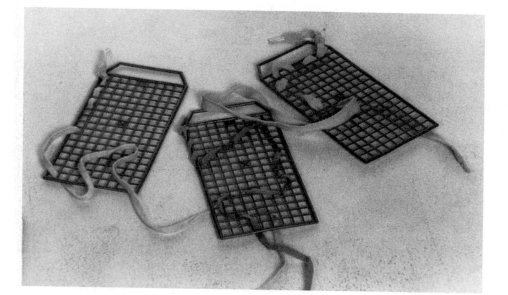

Let's Lace

STRATEGIES:

_____

_____

_____

_____

_____

_____

_____

_____

DEVELOPMENT:

_____

_____

_____

_____

_____

_____

_____

_____

_____

_____

VARIATIONS:

_____

_____

_____

_____

_____

_____

_____

_____

_____

_____

_____

Bear in a Chair Color Match

DEVELOPMENTAL LEVELS: 3–5 Years

AREAS OF DEVELOPMENT: Cognitive, Physical, Social

BENEFITS TO CHILD: Eye-hand coordination; partner play; mathematics; fine motor development; one-to-one correspondence

MATERIALS:

- Box lid (11" × 17")
- 24 plastic tops (milk, juice, water, and so forth—6 green, 6 yellow, 5 blue, 7 red)
- 24 small counting bears (6 green, 6 yellow, 5 blue, 7 red)
- Hot glue gun and glue sticks

HOW TO MAKE:

- Use hot glue to attach plastic tops to box lid (6 rows with 4 in each row in a random mix of colors).

3–5 Years   ✂   **69**

Bear in a Chair
Color Match

STRATEGIES:

_____
_____
_____
_____
_____
_____
_____
_____

DEVELOPMENT:

_____
_____
_____
_____
_____
_____
_____
_____
_____
_____

VARIATIONS:

_____
_____
_____
_____
_____
_____
_____
_____
_____
_____

Primary/Secondary Color Match

DEVELOPMENTAL LEVELS: 3–5 Years

AREAS OF DEVELOPMENT: Cognitive, Physical

BENEFITS TO CHILD: Visual discrimination; eye-hand coordination; fine motor development; independence

MATERIALS:

- ⊕ Wood strip (paint stir stick or thin 14" × 1" strip of board or 12" ruler)
- ⊕ 5 clothespins
- ⊕ Permanent markers (blue, red, green, orange, yellow, purple)

HOW TO MAKE:

- ✂ Make 1⅛" wide color for each of the six colors on the wood strip.
- ✂ Color each clip area (below metal) to match each of the six colors on the wood strip.

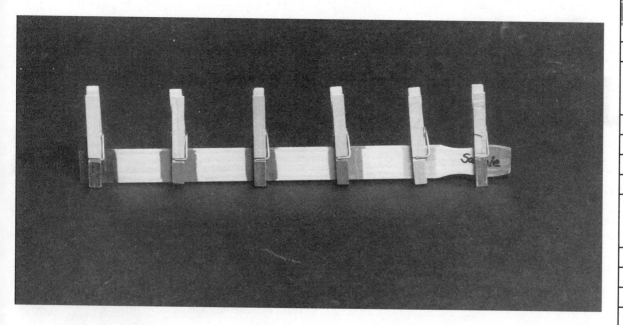

Primary/Secondary Color Match

STRATEGIES:

_____
_____
_____
_____
_____
_____
_____
_____
_____

DEVELOPMENT:

_____
_____
_____
_____
_____
_____
_____
_____
_____
_____

VARIATIONS:

_____
_____
_____
_____
_____
_____
_____
_____
_____
_____

Count the Corks

DEVELOPMENTAL LEVELS: 3–5 Years

AREAS OF DEVELOPMENT: Cognitive, Physical

BENEFITS TO CHILD: Eye-hand coordination; mathematics concepts; vocabulary building; fine motor skills

MATERIALS:

- Plastic shoe box with lid
- 55 corks (½'' × ¾'')
- Tea infuser with handle
- 10 clear plastic cups (8 oz)
- Self-adhesive plastic numbers (1 to 10)
- Water

HOW TO MAKE:

- Attach a number to each cup.
- Store corks, cups, and strainer in shoe box.
- Place 2'' of water in shoebox

How many corks can you count?

Count the Corks

STRATEGIES:

_____
_____
_____
_____
_____
_____
_____
_____
_____

DEVELOPMENT:

_____
_____
_____
_____
_____
_____
_____
_____
_____
_____
_____

VARIATIONS:

_____
_____
_____
_____
_____
_____
_____
_____
_____
_____
_____

Car Tracks

DEVELOPMENTAL LEVELS: 3–5 Years

AREAS OF DEVELOPMENT: Cognitive, Physical

BENEFITS TO CHILD: Fine motor development; eye-hand coordination; visual discrimination

MATERIALS:

- Corrugated cardboard (10" × 17")
- Colored self-adhesive plastic tape (¾" to 1½" width; 6' to 10' length)
- Small cars
- Colored string (long enough for car to move over all of track)
- Scissors
- Hole punch

HOW TO MAKE:

- Place tape on cardboard (on both sides) to make road tracks for car.
- Punch hole 1" from edge of cardboard.
- Attach string (color of road and car) to car and cardboard using appropriate length for car to run on road (but no longer for safety).

Car Tracks

STRATEGIES:

_____

_____

_____

_____

_____

_____

_____

_____

DEVELOPMENT:

_____

_____

_____

_____

_____

_____

_____

_____

_____

_____

VARIATIONS:

_____

_____

_____

_____

_____

_____

_____

_____

_____

_____

_____

_____

Sticker Match

DEVELOPMENTAL LEVELS: 3–5 Years

AREAS OF DEVELOPMENT: Cognitive, Physical, Social

BENEFITS TO CHILD: Language development; eye-hand coordination; cooperative play; mathematics concepts—one-to-one correspondence, matching

MATERIALS:

- Pizza box (15″)
- 16 canning lids
- Hot glue gun and glue sticks
- Pairs of pictures of shapes, foods, dots, and numbers
- Clear self-adhesive plastic or laminate
- White construction paper or cardboard (sixteen 2″ squares)

Sticker Match

HOW TO MAKE:

- Attach pictures to squares and matching pictures to tops of lids.
- Cover picture squares with clear self-adhesive plastic or laminate.
- Attach lids with hot glue to inside of pizza box in 4 rows of 4 each, approximately 1½" apart.
- Cut magnetic tape into 1" pieces and attach to back of squares.

STRATEGIES:

DEVELOPMENT:

VARIATIONS:

Individual Chalkboards

DEVELOPMENTAL LEVELS: 3–5 Years

AREAS OF DEVELOPMENT: Cognitive, Physical

BENEFITS TO CHILD: Creativity; fine motor development

MATERIALS:

- Detergent container (5.5 lb box with handle over top)
- 10 corrugated cardboard pieces (7" × 8½")
- Chalkboard paint
- 2" Velcro
- Paintbrush
- Chalk (variety of colors)
- 6" flannel cloth squares or erasers

Individual Chalkboards

HOW TO MAKE:

- ✂ Wash detergent box with disinfectant solution and dry thoroughly.

- ✂ Paint cardboard pieces on both sides with chalkboard paint (2 coats of paint).

- ✂ Cover detergent container with colored self-adhesive plastic or paint.

- ✂ Attach Velcro to inside of lid and back of eraser.

- ✂ Store eraser, chalk, and chalkboards in detergent container.

STRATEGIES:

_____

_____

_____

_____

_____

_____

DEVELOPMENT:

_____

_____

_____

_____

_____

_____

_____

_____

VARIATIONS:

_____

_____

_____

_____

_____

_____

_____

Clothes/Animal Sort

DEVELOPMENTAL LEVELS: 3–5 Years

AREAS OF DEVELOPMENT: Cognitive, Physical, Social

BENEFITS TO CHILD: Fine motor development; cooperative play; connect
words with pictures; visual discrimination

MATERIALS:

- Pizza box (15")
- 15 pictures of clothes and animals
  (a variety from magazines and
  catalogs)
- 2 peel-and-stick plastic hooks
- Clear self-adhesive plastic or
  laminate
- Black large tip permanent marker
- Ruler
- Hole punch
- Rubber cement

Clothes/Animal Sort

HOW TO MAKE:

- ✂ Draw a horizontal line across the middle of the inside of the pizza box with marker.

- ✂ Cover pictures with clear self-adhesive plastic or laminate.

- ✂ Write "Clothes" and attach 2 small pictures of clothing to upper left above horizontal line.

- ✂ Write "Animals" and attach 2 small pictures of animals to lower right below horizontal line.

- ✂ Attach hooks 4" from side of box beside "Clothes" and "Animals" words.

- ✂ Punch holes at center top of remaining pictures.

STRATEGIES:

_____
_____
_____
_____
_____
_____
_____
_____
_____

DEVELOPMENT:

_____
_____
_____
_____
_____
_____
_____
_____
_____

VARIATIONS:

_____
_____
_____
_____
_____
_____
_____

Food/Toy Sort

DEVELOPMENTAL LEVELS: 3–5 Years

AREAS OF DEVELOPMENT: Cognitive, Physical, Social

BENEFITS TO CHILD: Eye-hand coordination; visual discrimination; cooperative play; connect words with pictures

MATERIALS:

- Pizza box (13")
- 15 pictures of food and toys (a variety from magazines and catalogs)
- 2 self-adhesive plastic hooks
- Clear contact or laminate
- Black large tip permanent marker
- Ruler
- Hole punch
- Rubber cement

Food/Toy Sort

HOW TO MAKE:

- ✄ Draw a horizontal line across the middle of the inside of the pizza box.

- ✄ Write "Food" and attach 2 small pictures of food to upper left above horizontal line.

- ✄ Write "Toys" and attach 2 small pictures of toys to lower right below horizontal line.

- ✄ Attach hooks 4" from side of box beside "Food" and "Toy" words.

- ✄ Punch hole at center top of remaining pictures.

STRATEGIES:

_____
_____
_____
_____
_____
_____
_____

DEVELOPMENT:

_____
_____
_____
_____
_____
_____
_____

VARIATIONS:

_____
_____
_____
_____
_____
_____
_____
_____

Fish, Ducks, Etc.

DEVELOPMENTAL LEVELS: 3–5 Years

AREAS OF DEVELOPMENT: Cognitive, Physical, Social

BENEFITS TO CHILD: Sensory experience; visual discrimination; eye-hand coordination; cooperative play

MATERIALS:

- 2 plastic 1-cup measuring cups
- 2 plastic dishwashing tubs
- 3' long plastic gutter
- Small plastic colored ducks, fish, whales, and so forth that float
- 6" Velcro
- Water

HOW TO MAKE:

- Purchase items.
- Sand edges of gutter.
- Put Velcro on underside of gutter and on edges of tubs.
- Place 2" of water in tubs.

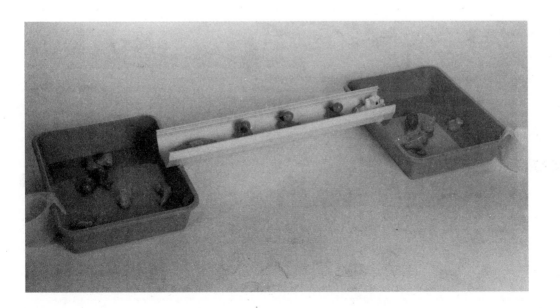

Age Level (Years)

2

3

4

5

6

7

8

Fish, Ducks, Etc.

STRATEGIES:

_____
_____
_____
_____
_____
_____
_____
_____
_____

DEVELOPMENT:

_____
_____
_____
_____
_____
_____
_____
_____
_____

VARIATIONS:

_____
_____
_____
_____
_____
_____
_____
_____
_____
_____

See Red

DEVELOPMENTAL LEVELS: 3–5 Years

AREAS OF DEVELOPMENT: Cognitive, Physical

BENEFITS TO CHILD: Sensory experience; stimulates curiosity; develops observation skills

MATERIALS:

- Box (7¼" × 7¼" × 3")
- 2 pieces of acetate report cover (3" × 7")
- Duct tape
- Hot glue gun and glue sticks
- Utility knife

HOW TO MAKE:

- Cut oval hole (3" × 7") in two opposite sides of box.
- Tape and hot glue the acetate pieces to inside of box to cover oval openings.
- Seal box with hot glue.
- Place duct tape over closures.

See Red

STRATEGIES:

_____
_____
_____
_____
_____
_____
_____
_____
_____

DEVELOPMENT:

_____
_____
_____
_____
_____
_____
_____
_____
_____
_____

VARIATIONS:

_____
_____
_____
_____
_____
_____
_____
_____
_____
_____
_____

From the Sea

DEVELOPMENTAL LEVELS: 3–5 Years

AREAS OF DEVELOPMENT: Cognitive, Physical, Social

BENEFITS TO CHILD: Eye-hand coordination; fine motor development; cooperative play; sensory experience

MATERIALS:

- 2 plastic tongs
- Fabric bolt
- Wallpaper wetting tray (32½" × 7½" × 4½")
- Colored self-adhesive plastic or laminate (20" × 36")
- 18" Velcro
- Ten 5" sharks
- Water

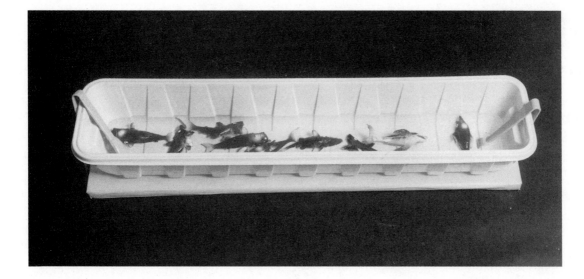

From the Sea

HOW TO MAKE:

✂ Cover fabric bolt with colored self-adhesive plastic or laminate.

✂ Attach four ½" strips of Velcro to fabric bolt at 3" and 6" from each end and loop side on bottom of tray in four places to match hook side.

✂ Place 3½" water in tray.

✂ Place sharks in tray.

STRATEGIES:

_____
_____
_____
_____
_____
_____
_____

DEVELOPMENT:

_____
_____
_____
_____
_____
_____
_____

VARIATIONS:

_____
_____
_____
_____
_____
_____
_____
_____
_____

Number Dots

DEVELOPMENTAL LEVELS: 3–5 Years

AREAS OF DEVELOPMENT: Cognitive, Physical

BENEFITS TO CHILD: Mathematics concepts—sequencing; eye-hand coordination; fine motor development

MATERIALS:

- Fabric bolt
- Self-adhesive plastic paper (18" × 28")
- 8 peel-and-stick plastic hooks
- 8 self-adhesive dot labels (numbers 1 to 8)
- 8 margarine tub lids
- 8 peel-and-stick plastic numbers (numbers 1 to 8)
- Permanent marker

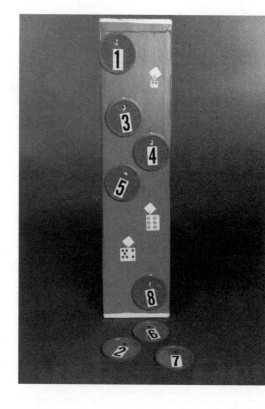

Number Dots

HOW TO MAKE:

- Cover fabric bolt.
- Attach plastic hooks to fabric bolt.
- Place dot labels below hooks (numbers 1 to 8).
- Make hole in lids.
- Place numbers on lids.
- Write number words in English and/or Spanish on back of lids.

STRATEGIES:

DEVELOPMENT:

VARIATIONS:

Felt Box

DEVELOPMENTAL LEVELS: 3–5 Years

AREAS OF DEVELOPMENT: Cognitive, Physical, Social

BENEFITS TO CHILD: Creativity; multicultural experience; language development; eye-hand coordination

MATERIALS:

- Box with handle (10'' × 7¼'' × 20½''), e.g., diaper, detergent
- Green felt (9'' × 12'')
- Red felt (21'' × 36'')
- Felt family (purchased)
- Orange felt for pumpkin (10½'' × 9'')
- Felt for fish (yellow, orange, purple, red; 7'' × 9'' each)
- Felt for shapes (red, blue, yellow, green; 4½'' × 9'' each for circles, squares, and triangles)
- Hot glue gun and glue sticks
- Disinfectant solution (1 tablespoon chlorine bleach mixed in 1 quart of water)
- Newspaper
- Scissors
- Clear Tape

Felt Box

HOW TO MAKE:

- ✄ Clean box with disinfectant and stuff tightly with newspaper.

- ✄ Tape box closed and attach red felt to all sides of box with hot glue.

- ✄ Attach green felt to top and bottom of box with hot glue.

- ✄ Cut items from felt.

STRATEGIES:

_____

_____

_____

_____

_____

_____

_____

_____

DEVELOPMENT:

_____

_____

_____

_____

_____

_____

_____

_____

VARIATIONS:

_____

_____

_____

_____

_____

_____

_____

_____

Top Sequencing

DEVELOPMENTAL LEVELS: 3–5 Years

AREAS OF DEVELOPMENT: Cognitive, Physical

BENEFITS TO CHILD: Mathematics concepts; eye-hand coordination; fine motor development; emergent literacy

MATERIALS:

- Fabric bolt
- 15 bottle tops (milk, juice; 1 yellow, 2 orange, 3 green, 4 red, 5 blue)
- 7½" Velcro (½" for each top)
- Small margarine tub (for storage of tops)
- Self-adhesive plastic (red or blue 20" × 36" pieces)
- Hot glue gun and glue sticks
- Disinfectant (1 tablespoon chlorine bleach in 1 quart water)

Top Sequencing

HOW TO MAKE:

- Clean tops with disinfectant and cover fabric bolt with self-adhesive plastic.
- Cut Velcro into ½" pieces.
- Attach one side of Velcro to bottle tops and other side of Velcro to fabric bolt for numbers 1 to 5.
- Write number words on fabric bolt (one to five).
- Hot glue margarine tub to fabric bolt.

STRATEGIES:

_____
_____
_____
_____
_____
_____
_____
_____
_____

DEVELOPMENT:

_____
_____
_____
_____
_____
_____
_____
_____
_____

VARIATIONS:

_____
_____
_____
_____
_____
_____
_____
_____

Zipper Book

DEVELOPMENTAL LEVELS: 3–5 Years

AREAS OF DEVELOPMENT: Cognitive, Physical

BENEFITS TO CHILD: Language development; visual discrimination; creativity

MATERIALS:

- Fabric book (10" × 12") with blue denim cover and 3 black felt pages (9" × 11½")

- Page 1: Shapes—2 blue 4" squares; 2 white 3" circles; 2 orange 3" triangles; 2 yellow 2" × 3" rectangles; 2 red 3" octagons; 2 green 2⅛" × 3" ovals

- Page 2: Bears—2 of each color and position; white, red, yellow, orange, blue, green

- Page 3: Animals—2 yellow ducks, 2 white rabbits, 2 blue birds, 2 orange jack-o-lanterns, 2 red hearts, 2 white turkeys

- Eighteen 1" Velcro pieces

- Glue

Zipper Book

HOW TO MAKE:

- Purchase or make book, shapes, and other items from denim and felt.
- Attach one of each item on felt page with glue.
- Attach hook piece of Velcro to each glued-on item.
- Attach loop piece of Velcro to matching "loose" felt piece.

STRATEGIES:

_____
_____
_____
_____
_____
_____
_____
_____

DEVELOPMENT:

_____
_____
_____
_____
_____
_____
_____

VARIATIONS:

_____
_____
_____
_____
_____
_____
_____
_____

Hippo Color Match

DEVELOPMENTAL LEVELS: 3–5 Years

AREAS OF DEVELOPMENT: Cognitive, Physical, Social

BENEFITS TO CHILD: Eye-hand coordination; visual discrimination; cooperative play; mathematics concepts—one-to-one correspondence

MATERIALS:

- File folder
- Clear self-adhesive plastic or laminate
- 8" sticky back Velcro
- 6 permanent wide tip markers (black, red, blue, yellow, green, orange)

- 16 round plastic markers (1⅛" diameter: 3 green, 4 red, 3 blue, 3 orange, 3 yellow)
- White construction paper (9" × 11½")
- Rubber cement

Hippo Color Match

HOW TO MAKE:

- ✂ Draw hippo on white paper using black marker.

- ✂ Draw and color circles to match plastic markers.

- ✂ Attach white paper with rubber cement to inside of folder.

- ✂ Cover folder on all sides with clear self-adhesive plastic or laminate.

- ✂ Cut Velcro into ½" pieces and attach one side of Velcro to each marker and other side of Velcro to center of color circles in folder.

STRATEGIES:

_____

_____

_____

_____

_____

_____

_____

DEVELOPMENT:

_____

_____

_____

_____

_____

_____

_____

_____

VARIATIONS:

_____

_____

_____

_____

_____

_____

_____

A House for My Friends

DEVELOPMENTAL LEVELS: 3–5 Years

AREAS OF DEVELOPMENT: Cognitive, Physical, Social

BENEFITS TO CHILD: Cooperative play; emergent literacy

MATERIALS:

- Pizza box (13")
- Felt: 8" × 8" green; 12½" × 12½" red; one each 2" × 4" yellow, purple, blue, red, orange; 1¼" × 2½" gray
- Poem
  Little mouse, little mouse
  Are you in the (color) house?
  Little mouse, little mouse
  You are not in the (color) house.
- Fabric glue
- Black large tip permanent marker
- Fabric paint (various colors or black)

A House for My Friends

HOW TO MAKE:

- ✂ Glue green felt inside pizza box top.
- ✂ Write "A House for My Friends" at the top and draw a roof triangle above the green square.
- ✂ Glue red felt in bottom of pizza box.

- ✂ Use pattern and cut small house from 2" × 4" felt pieces.
- ✂ Draw door and windows using fabric paint.
- ✂ Cut mouse from 1¼" × 2½" felt.

STRATEGIES:

_____
_____
_____
_____
_____
_____
_____
_____
_____
_____

DEVELOPMENT:

_____
_____
_____
_____
_____
_____
_____
_____

VARIATIONS:

_____
_____
_____
_____
_____
_____
_____
_____

Shape Pockets

DEVELOPMENTAL LEVELS: 3–5 Years

AREAS OF DEVELOPMENT: Cognitive, Physical

BENEFITS TO CHILD: Discrimination; eye-hand coordination; shape concepts; visual discrimination

MATERIALS:

- Blue denim or canvas fabric (12" × 30")

- Red denim or canvas fabric (three 8" × 12" pieces; one 2" × 15" piece)

- Yellow nontoxic fabric paint

- Paintbrush

- 10 each circles, squares, and triangles (can be made of construction paper, tagboard, and so forth in various colors)

- Self-adhesive plastic or laminate

Shape Pockets

HOW TO MAKE:

- ✄ Hem blue fabric and attach 2 loops made from 2" × 15" red fabric to top corners.

- ✄ Use red fabric (8" × 12" pieces) to make 3 pockets and sew to blue fabric, 2½" between pockets with 4½" space at top.

- ✄ Write "Shapes" in top 4½" space with yellow paint.

- ✄ On pockets, paint 5½" square on top, 5½" triangle in the middle, and 5½" circle on bottom.

- ✄ Make circles, squares, and triangles and cover with self-adhesive plastic or laminate.

STRATEGIES:

_____
_____
_____
_____
_____
_____
_____

DEVELOPMENT:

_____
_____
_____
_____
_____
_____

VARIATIONS:

_____
_____
_____
_____
_____
_____

Vegetable Match Board

DEVELOPMENTAL LEVELS: 3–5 Years

AREAS OF DEVELOPMENT: Cognitive, Physical

BENEFITS TO CHILD: Mathematics concepts; eye-hand coordination; language development; fine and gross motor development

MATERIALS:

- Double thickness corrugated cardboard (6½" × 15")
- 4" sticky back Velcro
- 8 canning jar lids
- 16 pictures of vegetables (2 matching pictures of each— corn, broccoli, squash, celery, beans, carrots, lettuce, peas)
- Carpet knife
- Green self-adhesive plastic (15" × 17")

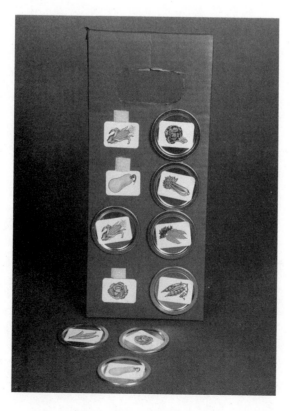

Vegetable Match Board

HOW TO MAKE:

✂ Cut 1½" × 3½" oblong hole in cardboard, 1¾" from top and 1½" from each side.

✂ Cover cardboard with self-adhesive plastic.

✂ Cut Velcro into 1" pieces and attach one side of Velcro to back of lids and other side of Velcro on cardboard in 2 rows of 4 approximately 3" apart.

✂ Attach one picture of each vegetable below piece of Velcro and matching picture of vegetable on front of each lid.

STRATEGIES:

_____
_____
_____
_____
_____
_____
_____
_____

DEVELOPMENT:

_____
_____
_____
_____
_____
_____
_____
_____

VARIATIONS:

_____
_____
_____
_____
_____
_____
_____

Wooden Numbers

DEVELOPMENTAL LEVELS: 3–5 Years

AREAS OF DEVELOPMENT: Cognitive, Physical

BENEFITS TO CHILD: Mathematics concepts; eye-hand coordination; visual discrimination

MATERIALS:

- Fabric bolt
- Scissors
- White self-adhesive plastic
- Blue nontoxic spray paint
- Six 3½" wooden numbers (1 to 6)
- Six 3" self-stick numbers (1 to 6)
- Twenty-one ¾" self-stick dots

- Six 1" pieces of Velcro
- Hot glue gun and glue sticks
- Clear self-adhesive plastic or laminate
- Six 3" × 3½" pieces white construction paper or cardboard

Wooden Numbers

HOW TO MAKE:

- Paint wooden numbers and let dry completely.
- Cover fabric bolt with white self-adhesive plastic.
- With hot glue attach wooden numbers along top of fabric bolt, 1½" to 2" apart.
- Attach Velcro below each wooden number.
- Attach each self-stick number to a 3" × 3½" card.
- Attach appropriate dots to back of each number card.
- Cover six cards with clear self-adhesive plastic or laminate.
- Attach 1" piece of Velcro to each card (on side with dots) near top.

STRATEGIES:

_____
_____
_____
_____
_____
_____
_____
_____

DEVELOPMENT:

_____
_____
_____
_____
_____
_____
_____
_____

VARIATIONS:

_____
_____
_____
_____
_____
_____
_____
_____

Match the Money

DEVELOPMENTAL LEVELS: 3–5 Years

AREAS OF DEVELOPMENT: Cognitive, Physical

BENEFITS TO CHILD: Mathematics concepts; one-to-one correspondence; fine motor development

MATERIALS:

- 8" duct tape
- Corrugated cardboard (19" × 27")
- Green tagboard (18" × 24")
- Money: $1, $5, $10, and $20 bills
- Rubber cement
- 4" sticky back Velcro
- Clear self-adhesive plastic or laminate (28" × 100")

Match the Money

HOW TO MAKE:

- ✄ Enlarge money on photocopy machine, making two copies of each.

- ✄ Attach one copy of each bill to green tagboard using rubber cement.

- ✄ Using clear self-adhesive plastic, cover tagboard with attached money and copies of $1, $5, $10, and $20 bills.

- ✄ Attach 1" piece of hook side of Velcro to each bill on green tagboard.

- ✄ Attach 1" piece of loop side of Velcro to copy of $1, $5, $10, and $20 bills.

- ✄ Attach green tagboard to corrugated cardboard at top using duct tape.

STRATEGIES:

_____
_____
_____
_____
_____
_____
_____

DEVELOPMENT:

_____
_____
_____
_____
_____
_____
_____

VARIATIONS:

_____
_____
_____
_____
_____
_____

Shapes That Are Alike

DEVELOPMENTAL LEVELS: 3–6 Years

AREAS OF DEVELOPMENT: Cognitive, Physical

BENEFITS TO CHILD: Eye-hand coordination; classification; fine motor development; concept development; sequencing; visual discrimination.

MATERIALS:

⊕ Felt—all one color or several colors to make squares, circles, triangles, and rectangles in a variety of sizes.

HOW TO MAKE:

✂ Make large size of each shape.

✂ Make each shape in a variety of smaller sizes.

Shapes That Are Alike

STRATEGIES:

_____
_____
_____
_____
_____
_____
_____
_____
_____
_____

DEVELOPMENT:

_____
_____
_____
_____
_____
_____
_____
_____
_____
_____
_____

VARIATIONS:

_____
_____
_____
_____
_____
_____
_____
_____
_____
_____
_____

Car License Plate

DEVELOPMENTAL LEVELS: 3–6 Years

AREAS OF DEVELOPMENT: Cognitive, Physical

BENEFITS TO CHILD: Sensory experience; fine motor development; emergent literacy

MATERIALS:

- ⊛ 2 or more old license plates
- ⊛ Manila paper or butcher paper (12" × 18")
- ⊛ Large crayons—various colors, some with paper removed from them

HOW TO MAKE:

- ✂ Collect materials.

Car License Plate

STRATEGIES:

_____
_____
_____
_____
_____
_____
_____

DEVELOPMENT:

_____
_____
_____
_____
_____
_____
_____
_____
_____
_____

VARIATIONS:

_____
_____
_____
_____
_____
_____
_____
_____
_____
_____

Circles and Circles

DEVELOPMENTAL LEVELS: 3–6 Years

AREAS OF DEVELOPMENT: Cognitive, Physical

BENEFITS TO CHILD: Eye-hand coordination; seriation; fine motor development; creativity

MATERIALS:

- 6 clear plastic plant saucers—4", 6", 8", 10", 12" and 14" diameters
- Washable, nontoxic markers
- Terry washcloth or scrap of fabric
- Large pizza box for storing plastic plant saucers
- 2 detergent bottle lids for storing materials

HOW TO MAKE:

- ✂ Purchase or collect items.

Circles and Circles

STRATEGIES:

_____
_____
_____
_____
_____
_____
_____
_____
_____
_____

DEVELOPMENT:

_____
_____
_____
_____
_____
_____
_____
_____
_____
_____

VARIATIONS:

_____
_____
_____
_____
_____
_____
_____
_____
_____
_____

Pick and Count the Pom-poms

DEVELOPMENTAL LEVELS: 3–6 years

AREAS OF DEVELOPMENT: Cognitive, Physical, Social

BENEFITS TO CHILD: Eye-hand coordination; mathematics concepts; cooperative play

MATERIALS:

- Melon tray with 4 sections for sorting
- 2 mini meatballers
- 1½" pom-poms—10 of each color: red, green, purple, black
- 14" clear plastic plant saucer

HOW TO MAKE:

- ✂ Collect items listed.

Pick and Count the Pom-poms

STRATEGIES:

DEVELOPMENT:

VARIATIONS:

Transition Box

DEVELOPMENTAL LEVELS: 3–6 Years

AREAS OF DEVELOPMENT: Cognitive, Physical, Social

BENEFITS TO CHILD: Fine motor development; cooperative play

MATERIALS:

- Box with handle opening (25" × 10½" × 9")
- Colored self-adhesive plastic or laminate (36" × 45")
- Assorted items:
  - "Car Tracks" (p. 71)
  - Magic slate (purchase)
  - Magnetic Ball (purchase)
  - Golden Goose Game (purchase)
  - Basketball (purchase)
  - Metal cars (purchase)
  - Lacing items—butterfly, circle, gingerbread boy, square (make and/or purchase)
  - "Let's Lace" (p. 63)
  - "Individual Chalkboards" (p. 75)

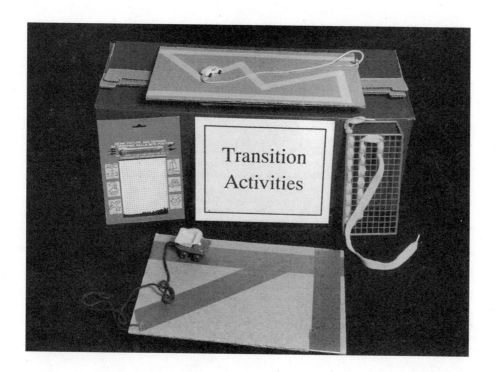

Transition Box

HOW TO MAKE:

- ✄ Cover box with self-adhesive plastic or laminate.
- ✄ Collect items and place in box.

STRATEGIES:

_____
_____
_____
_____
_____
_____
_____
_____
_____
_____

DEVELOPMENT:

_____
_____
_____
_____
_____
_____
_____
_____
_____
_____
_____
_____

VARIATIONS:

_____
_____
_____
_____
_____
_____
_____
_____
_____
_____

Sink or Float

DEVELOPMENTAL LEVELS: 3–6 Years

AREAS OF DEVELOPMENT: Cognitive, Physical

BENEFITS TO CHILD: Concept development; emergent literacy; sensory experience

MATERIALS:

- Large double dish for feeding pets
- Black wide tip permanent marker
- Objects that sink or float (cork, clothespins, Ping-Pong balls, spools, metal clips, and so forth)
- Ziploc bag

HOW TO MAKE:

- ✂ Store objects in Ziploc bag.
- ✂ Write "sink" on one side of the dish and "float" on the other side of the dish.
- ✂ Fill each side with 2" water.

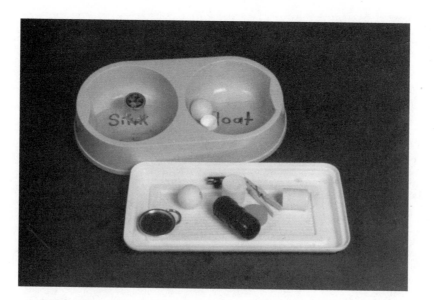

Sink or Float

STRATEGIES:

_____
_____
_____
_____
_____
_____
_____
_____
_____

DEVELOPMENT:

_____
_____
_____
_____
_____
_____
_____
_____
_____
_____
_____

VARIATIONS:

_____
_____
_____
_____
_____
_____
_____
_____
_____
_____
_____
_____

Catch the Clips

DEVELOPMENTAL LEVELS: 3–6 Years

AREAS OF DEVELOPMENT: Cognitive, Physical, Social

BENEFITS TO CHILD: Eye-hand coordination; sensory experience; science—magnet effect; mathematics concepts; color recognition, language development

MATERIALS:

- Wand magnet
- Clear plastic 1-gallon jug
- 2" colored paper clips—10 pink, 11 yellow, 19 blue, 19 white, 18 purple, 12 green, 12 red
- 2 pieces green tagboard (6" × 10")
- Clear self-adhesive plastic or laminate (11" × 25")
- Black and red markers

Catch the Clips

HOW TO MAKE:

- ✂ Collect items.
- ✂ Write "Catch the Clips" on one green tagboard piece and "Can you guess how many clips are in the bottle?" on the other green tagboard piece.
- ✂ Cover tagboard with clear self-adhesive plastic or laminate.

STRATEGIES:

_____
_____
_____
_____
_____
_____
_____
_____
_____

DEVELOPMENT:

_____
_____
_____
_____
_____
_____
_____
_____
_____

VARIATIONS:

_____
_____
_____
_____
_____
_____
_____
_____
_____

How Many Balls Can You Count?

DEVELOPMENTAL LEVELS: 3–6 Years

AREAS OF DEVELOPMENT: Cognitive, Physical, Social

BENEFITS TO CHILD: Mathematics concepts; eye-hand coordination; cooperative play; fine motor development

MATERIALS:

- Pizza box (15")
- 20 bottle tops (milk, juice, water, and so forth)
- 2 tea strainer diffusers
- Twenty 1" balls
- Hot glue gun and glue sticks
- Black wide tip permanent marker

HOW TO MAKE:

- Write "How many balls can you count?" inside top.
- Attach bottle tops to inside of box in 4 rows of 5 each, with 1" to 2" between them.

How Many Balls Can You Count?

STRATEGIES:

_____
_____
_____
_____
_____
_____
_____
_____
_____
_____
_____

DEVELOPMENT:

_____
_____
_____
_____
_____
_____
_____
_____
_____
_____
_____

VARIATIONS:

_____
_____
_____
_____
_____
_____
_____
_____
_____
_____

Crabs and Crawfish

DEVELOPMENTAL LEVELS: 3–6 Years

AREAS OF DEVELOPMENT: Cognitive, Physical, Social

BENEFITS TO CHILD: Language development; emergent literacy; eye-hand coordination; sensory experience; mathematics concepts

MATERIALS:

- 4 red plastic crabs
- 6 red plastic crawfish
- Plastic tub (4" × 18" × 14")
- 4-cup plastic container with lid
- Sand
- Water
- Plastic scoop
- Crab notepad or cutout

HOW TO MAKE:

✂ Write on crabs:

    (1)   "Catch a crab"

    (2)   "How many crabs?"

    (3)   "Catch a crawfish"

    (4)   "How many crawfish?"

✂ Place sand and 2" of water in plastic tub.

Crabs and Crawfish

STRATEGIES:

_____
_____
_____
_____
_____
_____
_____
_____
_____
_____

DEVELOPMENT:

_____
_____
_____
_____
_____
_____
_____
_____
_____
_____

VARIATIONS:

_____
_____
_____
_____
_____
_____
_____
_____
_____
_____
_____

Catch the Frogs

DEVELOPMENTAL LEVELS: 3–6 Years

AREAS OF DEVELOPMENT: Cognitive, Physical

BENEFITS TO CHILD: Sensory experience; mathematics concepts; eye-hand coordination; connect words with objects

MATERIALS:

- 3 to 4 quart clear plastic bowl
- 24 plastic frogs
- Aquarium fishnet
- Black permanent marker
- Yellow poster board (12″ × 18″)
- Clear self-adhesive plastic or laminate

HOW TO MAKE:

- Cut pond from poster board.
- Write "How many frogs are swimming?" on pond.
- Cover pond with clear self-adhesive plastic or laminate.
- Place frogs and 1 quart water in clear plastic bowl.

Catch the Frogs

STRATEGIES:

_____
_____
_____
_____
_____
_____
_____
_____
_____

DEVELOPMENT:

_____
_____
_____
_____
_____
_____
_____
_____
_____
_____
_____
_____

VARIATIONS:

_____
_____
_____
_____
_____
_____
_____
_____
_____
_____
_____

Snakes

DEVELOPMENTAL LEVELS: 3–6 Years

AREAS OF DEVELOPMENT: Cognitive, Physical, Social

BENEFITS TO CHILD: Eye-hand coordination; cooperative play; mathematics concepts; sensory experiences; fine motor development; language development; creativity

MATERIALS:

- Paint tray (13" × 16" × 4")
- Yellow tagboard (12" × 18")
- Black marker
- 2 metal tongs
- 1 quart plastic container with lid
- Sand
- Water
- 12 plastic snakes
- Snake puppet
- Plastic or fabric storage bags

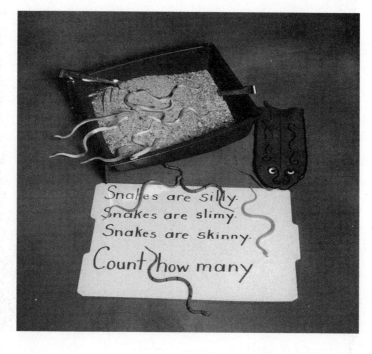

Snakes are silly.
Snakes are slimy.
Snakes are skinny.
Count how many

Snakes

HOW TO MAKE:

- ✂ Put sand, 3½" water, and snakes in tray.

- ✂ On yellow tagboard print with marker:

  Snakes are silly.
  Snakes are slimy.
  Snakes are skinny.
  Count how many.

- ✂ Cover yellow tagboard with clear self-adhesive plastic or laminate.

- ✂ Make or purchase snake puppet.

STRATEGIES:

_____

_____

_____

_____

_____

_____

_____

_____

DEVELOPMENT:

_____

_____

_____

_____

_____

_____

VARIATIONS:

_____

_____

_____

_____

_____

_____

_____

Unflannel Flannel Board

DEVELOPMENTAL LEVELS: 3–6 Years

AREAS OF DEVELOPMENT: Cognitive, Physical, Social

BENEFITS TO CHILD: Mathematics concepts; sorting; language development; eye-hand coordination; sequencing

MATERIALS:

- ⊛ Brown heavy corduroy placemat (18" × 13½")

- ⊛ Felt items—1 dog, 2 cats, 3 squirrels, 4 frogs, 5 pumpkins (purchase or make)

- ⊛ 3" felt numbers (1 to 5; purchase or make)

- ⊛ Fabric storage bag

HOW TO MAKE:

- ✂ Purchase or make placemat.

- ✂ Purchase or make felt items and numbers.

- ✂ Keep together in storage bag.

Unflannel Flannel Board

STRATEGIES:

_____

_____

_____

_____

_____

_____

_____

_____

DEVELOPMENT:

_____

_____

_____

_____

_____

_____

_____

_____

_____

VARIATIONS:

_____

_____

_____

_____

_____

_____

_____

_____

_____

_____

_____

Individual Flannel Boards

DEVELOPMENTAL LEVELS: 3–6 Years

AREAS OF DEVELOPMENT: Cognitive, Physical, Social

BENEFITS TO CHILD: Mathematics development; language development; independence; cooperative play

MATERIALS:

- Box with attached lid (7" × 2¾" × 9")
- Colored self-adhesive plastic or laminate (9" × 26")
- Colored felt (9" × 26")
- 3" felt numbers (1 to 7)
- Felt items: two 8" × 8" green trees, three 2½" × 6" red ladybugs, four 5" × 6" white snowmen, five 6" × 8" yellow ducks, six 7" × 9" white rabbits, seven 6" × 9" orange pumpkin cut outs
- Black permanent marker
- Scissors
- Glue

Individual Flannel Boards

HOW TO MAKE:

✂ Using glue to attach, line inside of box with felt.

✂ Cover outside of box with colored self-adhesive plastic.

✂ Purchase or make numbers and items.

STRATEGIES:

_____

_____

_____

_____

_____

_____

_____

_____

_____

DEVELOPMENT:

_____

_____

_____

_____

_____

_____

_____

_____

VARIATIONS:

_____

_____

_____

_____

_____

_____

_____

_____

One to Ten

Age Level (Years)

2

3

4

5

6

7

8

DEVELOPMENTAL LEVELS: 3–6 Years

AREAS OF DEVELOPMENT: Cognitive, Physical

BENEFITS TO CHILD: Mathematics concepts; eye-hand coordination; fine motor control; visual discrimination

MATERIALS:

- 10 plastic powdered drink containers (2½'' × 6½'')
- 4½'' black self-adhesive numbers (1 to 10)
- 55 tongue depressors
- Red spray paint
- Disinfectant solution (1 tablespoon chlorine bleach in 1 quart water)
- Box with handle for storage

One to Ten

HOW TO MAKE:

- ✄ Wash drink containers with disinfectant solution.
- ✄ Paint tongue depressors and dry thoroughly.
- ✄ Attach numbers to drink containers.

STRATEGIES:

_____
_____
_____
_____
_____
_____
_____
_____

DEVELOPMENT:

_____
_____
_____
_____
_____
_____
_____
_____
_____
_____

VARIATIONS:

_____
_____
_____
_____
_____
_____
_____
_____
_____

Bear Color Match

DEVELOPMENTAL LEVELS: 3–6 Years

AREAS OF DEVELOPMENT: Cognitive, Physical, Social

BENEFITS TO CHILD: Mathematics concepts; cooperative play; fine motor development; eye-hand coordination; visual discrimination

MATERIALS:

- Colored bears (40 red, 40 blue, 40 yellow, 40 green)

- Poster board (one 8½" × 17" piece; four 8" × 10" pieces; one 5" × 6" piece)

- Clear self-adhesive plastic or laminate (30" × 36")

- ¾" self-adhesive dots (32 red, 24 blue, 26 yellow, 25 green)

- Large envelope for storage of boards

- ½-gallon clear plastic container with lid for storage of bears

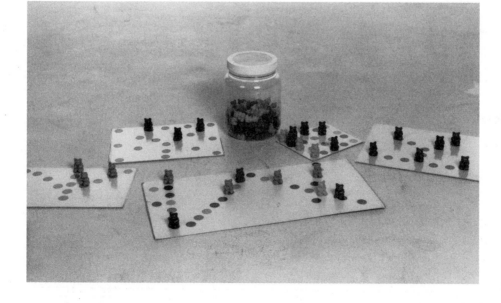

Bear Color Match

HOW TO MAKE:

✄ Attach self-adhesive dots to boards (one 8½" × 17"—four colors; one 5" × 6"—four colors; four 8" × 10"—1 color on each board)

✄ Cover cards on both sides with clear self-adhesive plastic or laminate.

STRATEGIES:

_____

_____

_____

_____

_____

_____

_____

_____

DEVELOPMENT:

_____

_____

_____

_____

_____

_____

_____

_____

_____

_____

_____

VARIATIONS:

_____

_____

_____

_____

_____

_____

_____

_____

_____

Bear Color Match Two

DEVELOPMENTAL LEVELS: 3–6 Years

AREAS OF DEVELOPMENT: Cognitive, Physical, Social

BENEFITS TO CHILD: Mathematics concepts; cooperative play; fine motor development; eye-hand coordination; visual discrimination

MATERIALS:

- Colored bears (40 red, 40 blue, 40 yellow, 40 green)
- ½-gallon clear container with lid
- 4 poster board pieces (9" × 12")
- Wrapping paper (black background with red, yellow, blue, green dots; 10" × 34")
- Glue
- Scissors
- Clear self-adhesive plastic or laminate

Bear Color Match Two

HOW TO MAKE:

- ✂ Cut 10" × 8½" pieces of wrapping paper.
- ✂ Attach wrapping paper to poster board.
- ✂ Cover both sides of poster boards with clear self-adhesive plastic or laminate.

STRATEGIES:

_____
_____
_____
_____
_____
_____
_____
_____

DEVELOPMENT:

_____
_____
_____
_____
_____
_____
_____
_____
_____

VARIATIONS:

_____
_____
_____
_____
_____
_____
_____
_____

Key Match

DEVELOPMENTAL LEVELS: 3–6 Years

AREAS OF DEVELOPMENT: Cognitive, Physical

BENEFITS TO CHILD: Visual discrimination; eye-hand coordination; seriation; one-to-one correspondence; fine motor development

MATERIALS:

- 11 keys (variety of sizes and shapes)
- Access to copy machine (if none available, outline keys)
- Tagboard (10½" × 13")
- Clear self-adhesive plastic or laminate (13½" × 22")
- Rubber cement
- Bag or box for key storage

Key Match

HOW TO MAKE:

- ✀ Arrange keys on copy machine and make 2 copies.

- ✀ Attach copied key sheets to tagboard with rubber cement, one sheet centered on each side.

- ✀ Cover both sides of tagboard with clear self-adhesive or laminate.

STRATEGIES:

_____
_____
_____
_____
_____
_____
_____
_____

DEVELOPMENT:

_____
_____
_____
_____
_____
_____
_____
_____

VARIATIONS:

_____
_____
_____
_____
_____
_____
_____
_____

Number Match

DEVELOPMENTAL LEVELS: 3–6 Years

AREAS OF DEVELOPMENT: Cognitive, Physical

BENEFITS TO CHILD: Mathematics concepts; eye-hand coordination; fine motor development; sequencing

MATERIALS:

- Box (5¾" × 8¾" × 2¾")
- Green self-adhesive plastic or laminate (9" × 18")
- Tongue depressors
- Knife
- Self-adhesive 1" numbers (two each of 0, 3, 4, 5, 6, 7, 8, 9; four each of 1, 2)

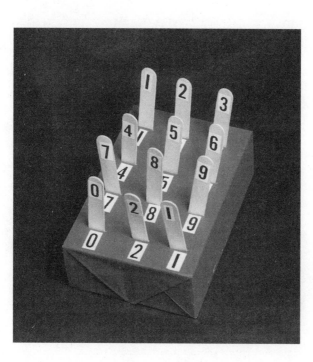

Number Match

HOW TO MAKE:

- ✂ Cover box with self-adhesive plastic or laminate.
- ✂ Cut twelve 1" slots in top of box (3 columns across approximately 1" apart; 4 rows down approximately 2" apart).
- ✂ Place self-adhesive numbers below slots.
- ✂ Place self-adhesive numbers on tongue depressors.

STRATEGIES:

_____
_____
_____
_____
_____
_____
_____
_____

DEVELOPMENT:

_____
_____
_____
_____
_____
_____
_____
_____

VARIATIONS:

_____
_____
_____
_____
_____
_____
_____

Mitten Flannel Board

DEVELOPMENTAL LEVELS: 3–6 Years

AREAS OF DEVELOPMENT: Cognitive, Physical

BENEFITS TO CHILD: Creativity; language development; visual discrimination

MATERIALS:

- Heavy cardboard (10" × 12")
- Light colored flannel fabric (35" × 11")
- Felt objects and numbers e.g., trees, story items, and so forth
- Sewing machine (or hand sewn)

HOW TO MAKE:

- Cut 11" × 25" piece of flannel for covering cardboard.
- Cut large mitten from 10" × 11" piece of flannel.
- Hem cuff edge of mitten.
- Turn under raw edges of mitten.
- Sew mitten to one side of large piece of flannel, leaving cuff edge open for adult or child's hand.

Mitten Flannel Board

STRATEGIES:

_____
_____
_____
_____
_____
_____
_____
_____
_____
_____

DEVELOPMENT:

_____
_____
_____
_____
_____
_____
_____
_____
_____
_____
_____

VARIATIONS:

_____
_____
_____
_____
_____
_____
_____
_____
_____
_____
_____
_____
_____

Hanging Around

DEVELOPMENTAL LEVELS: 3–6 Years

AREAS OF DEVELOPMENT: Cognitive, Physical, Social

BENEFITS TO CHILD: Mathematics development; eye-hand coordination; visual discrimination; cooperative play; language development

MATERIALS:

- Fabric bolt (8" × 30")
- Colored self-adhesive plastic or laminate (20" × 30")
- 5 plastic self-adhesive coat hooks (3" × 3¾")
- Black self-adhesive 2" numbers (1 to 5)

- 15 shower curtain hooks
- Fifteen 2" × 2⅜" vinyl pieces with holes at top
- Stickers or pictures (1 banana, 2 oranges, 3 cardinals, 4 clowns, 5 dinosaurs)

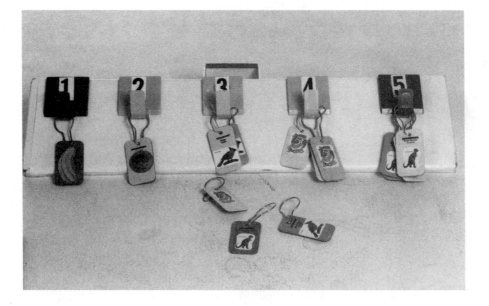

Hanging Around

HOW TO MAKE:

- Cover fabric bolt with colored self-adhesive plastic or laminate.
- Attach self-adhesive numbers to coat hooks.
- Attach coat hooks to the covered fabric bolt along top edge, 1½" from ends and approximately 3½" apart.
- Attach stickers or pictures to vinyl pieces.
- Attach shower curtain hook to each vinyl piece.

STRATEGIES:

_____
_____
_____
_____
_____
_____
_____
_____

DEVELOPMENT:

_____
_____
_____
_____
_____
_____
_____

VARIATIONS:

_____
_____
_____
_____
_____
_____
_____

Let's Fish

DEVELOPMENTAL LEVELS: 3–6 Years

AREAS OF DEVELOPMENT: Cognitive, Emotional, Physical, Social

BENEFITS TO CHILD: Cooperative play; sensory experience; eye-hand coordination; fine motor skills; visual discrimination

MATERIALS:

- Fabric bolt
- Colored self-adhesive plastic
- Clear plastic shoe box (18" × 18")
- Four ¾" metal washers
- Magnetic tape (½" × 15")
- Fifteen 2" to 3" fish from colored tagboard

- Sandpaper
- Dowel (¾" diameter; 20" length)
- 24" cord
- Construction paper (8" × 8")
- 2 visors
- 2 margarine tubs with lids
- Hot glue gun and glue sticks

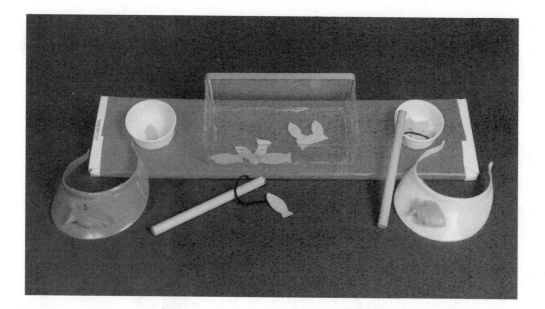

Let's Fish

HOW TO MAKE:

- ✂ Cover fabric bolt with colored self-adhesive plastic.

- ✂ Attach margarine tubs and shoe box to fabric bolt with hot glue, shoe box in center and tubs 3" from each end.

- ✂ Saw dowel into two 10" pieces and smooth edges with sandpaper.

- ✂ With hot glue, attach cord and a washer to one end of each dowel.

- ✂ Attach a washer to the other end of each cord.

- ✂ Cut out 15 fish from colored tagboard and cover with clear plastic adhesive or laminate.

- ✂ Cut magnetic tape into fifteen 1" pieces.

- ✂ Attach magnetic tape to each fish.

STRATEGIES:

_____
_____
_____
_____
_____
_____
_____
_____

DEVELOPMENT:

_____
_____
_____
_____
_____
_____
_____
_____

VARIATIONS:

_____
_____
_____
_____
_____

Wormy Apples

DEVELOPMENTAL LEVELS: 3–6 Years

AREAS OF DEVELOPMENT: Cognitive, Physical, Social

BENEFITS TO CHILD: Sensory experience; mathematics concepts; eye-hand coordination; cooperative play; connect words with objects

MATERIALS:

- 55 plastic worms
- Green poster board (12" × 18")
- 10 pieces red poster board (10" squares)
- Clear self-adhesive plastic or laminate
- Large self-adhesive plastic numbers (1 to 10)
- Hole punch
- Black wide tip permanent marker
- Plastic container with lid (½-gallon ice cream, peanut butter, and so forth)
- Duct tape

Wormy Apples

HOW TO MAKE:

✂ Write on green poster board "How many worms can you count?" and cut to make mat.

✂ Cut out 10 apples from red poster board.

✂ Attach numbers, one on each apple, or write numbers on apples using marker.

✂ Cover green mat and apples with clear self-adhesive plastic or laminate.

✂ Use hole punch to make holes in each apple to correspond with numbers.

✂ Cut opening in middle of plastic container lid (2½" × 3").

✂ Cover cut edges of lid with duct tape.

✂ Place worms in container.

STRATEGIES:

_____
_____
_____
_____
_____
_____
_____

DEVELOPMENT:

_____
_____
_____
_____
_____
_____

VARIATIONS:

_____
_____
_____
_____
_____
_____
_____

Frogs—Big and Little

DEVELOPMENTAL LEVELS: 3–6 Years

AREAS OF DEVELOPMENT: Cognitive, Physical, Social

BENEFITS TO CHILD: Mathematics concepts; eye-hand coordination; sensory experience; fine motor development; cooperative play

MATERIALS:

- Plastic tub (21″ top, 14″ bottom, 8½″ deep)
- 1 plastic frog placemat
- Small fishnet
- 2 plastic tongs
- 12 large plastic frogs
- 55 small plastic frogs
- 14″ clear plastic plant saucer
- 10 frog cutouts
- 3″ self-adhesive black numbers
- 15″ × 80″ clear self-adhesive plastic or laminate
- Large plastic frog
- 2 quarts of water

Frogs—Big and Little

HOW TO MAKE:

- ✂ Fill plastic tub for large frogs with 6" of water.

- ✂ Fill plant saucer for small frogs with 1" of water.

- ✂ Place numbers on frog cutouts.

STRATEGIES:

_____

_____

_____

_____

_____

_____

_____

_____

_____

DEVELOPMENT:

_____

_____

_____

_____

_____

_____

_____

_____

VARIATIONS:

_____

_____

_____

_____

_____

_____

_____

_____

Birds in a Tree

DEVELOPMENTAL LEVELS: 3–6 Years

AREAS OF DEVELOPMENT: Cognitive, Physical, Social

BENEFITS TO CHILD: Visual discrimination; matching; language development; mathematics concepts; one-to-one correspondence

MATERIALS:

- Corrugated cardboard (17" × 27")

- Tagboard: green (11" × 16"), purple (5" × 9"), brown (6" × 14"), blue (5" × 7")

- Plastic Wipes case

- Black marker

- Clear self-adhesive plastic or laminate (16" × 50")

- Bird stickers—sets of eight different birds

- Duct tape

Birds in a Tree

HOW TO MAKE:

- ✄ Cut tree top and trunk from tagboard.
- ✄ Attach one set of birds to tree top.
- ✄ Attach one set of birds to purple tagboard and cut apart.
- ✄ Write "How many birds are singing in the tree?" on blue tagboard.
- ✄ Cover all tagboard materials with clear self-adhesive plastic or laminate.
- ✄ Attach tree and "How many birds are singing in the tree?" to cardboard with duct tape.

STRATEGIES:

_____
_____
_____
_____
_____
_____
_____
_____
_____

DEVELOPMENT:

_____
_____
_____
_____
_____
_____
_____
_____
_____

VARIATIONS:

_____
_____
_____
_____
_____
_____
_____
_____

Count the Ducks

DEVELOPMENTAL LEVELS: 3–6 Years

AREAS OF DEVELOPMENT: Cognitive, Physical, Social

BENEFITS TO CHILD: Mathematics concepts; language development; eye-hand coordination; sensory experience; cooperative play

MATERIALS:

- Plastic round tub (21" top, 14" bottom, 8½" deep)
- 12 plastic floating ducks; 6" × 12"
- Tagboard: 2 green (12" × 18"), yellow (12" × 12")
- Water

- Black permanent marker
- ¾" self-stick black numbers (1 to 12)
- Clear self-adhesive plastic or laminate (12" × 90")
- 2 plastic or fabric storage bags

Count the Ducks

HOW TO MAKE:

- Fill plastic tub with 6" of water.

- Write "Count the ducks 1, 2, 3. How many ducks do you see?" on 12" × 18" green tagboard.

- Write "1, 2, 3 How many ducks do you see? Pick me up and match me." on 6" × 12" green tagboard.

- Cut 12 ducks from yellow tag-board and place one self-stick number on each.

- Cover all tagboard items with clear self-adhesive plastic or laminate.

- Write the numbers 1 to 12 on bottom of floating ducks.

STRATEGIES:

_____

_____

_____

_____

_____

_____

_____

_____

DEVELOPMENT:

_____

_____

_____

_____

_____

_____

_____

VARIATIONS:

_____

_____

_____

_____

_____

_____

Butterflies

DEVELOPMENTAL LEVELS: 3–6 Years

AREAS OF DEVELOPMENT: Cognitive, Physical, Social

BENEFITS TO CHILD: Eye-hand coordination; counting; matching objects; emergent literacy; cooperative play

MATERIALS:

- Ten 8″ × 10″ pieces of tagboard of various colors or large ready-made butterflies
- Ten 2″ × 3″ pieces of tagboard of various colors or small ready-made butterflies
- Black permanent marker
- 3½″ × 5″ self-adhesive or laminate numbers (1 to 10)
- 10 toilet paper rolls
- Solid color self-adhesive plastic or laminate (12″ × 25″)
- 55 plastic butterflies
- Clear self-adhesive plastic or laminate (20″ × 90″)
- Storage box (3″ × 12″ × 13″)
- Rubber cement
- Scissors

© 2001, Delmar

Butterflies

HOW TO MAKE:

- Cut out large butterflies from 8" × 10" tagboard.

- Attach a self-adhesive number to each.

- Cut out small butterflies from 2" × 3" tagboard.

- With marker write number word, one to ten, on each small butterfly.

- Attach each small butterfly to matching large numbered butterfly.

- Cover butterflies with clear self-adhesive plastic or laminate.

- Cover toilet paper rolls with solid color self-adhesive plastic.

- Make two 1" cuts opposite each other, on one end of toilet paper rolls.

STRATEGIES:

_____
_____
_____
_____
_____
_____
_____

DEVELOPMENT:

_____
_____
_____
_____
_____
_____

VARIATIONS:

_____
_____
_____
_____
_____
_____
_____

Pumpkin Patch Match

DEVELOPMENTAL LEVELS: 3–6 Years

AREAS OF DEVELOPMENT: Cognitive, Physical, Social

BENEFITS TO CHILD: Eye-hand coordination; classifying and sequencing; matching, mathematics concepts; cultural awareness

MATERIALS:

- Large box (14½" × 22" × 8")
- Wood-grain self-adhesive plastic (24" × 64")
- Black permanent marker
- 2" × 4½" black self-adhesive numbers (1 to 10)
- 10 plastic self-adhesive cup hooks
- Orange tagboard (10" × 140")
- Ninety ¾" diameter black self-adhesive dots
- Clear self-adhesive plastic or laminate (10" × 340")
- White poster board (5" × 14")

Pumpkin Patch Match

HOW TO MAKE:

- Cut out eighteen 4½" × 5" small pumpkins from orange tagboard.
- Using black marker, print number words one to ten on one side of small pumpkins and attach corresponding number of black dots to back of each.
- Make 10 large pumpkins from orange tag board.
- Attach 2" × 4½" numbers, 1 to 10, to large pumpkins and attach dots on back to correspond with each number.
- Write number words in Spanish (uno, dos, tres, cuatro, cinco, seis, siete, ocho) on 8 small pumpkins.
- Cover each pumpkin with clear self-adhesive plastic or laminate.
- Cover large box with wood-grain self-adhesive plastic.
- Attach cup hooks to sides of large box, 3 on 22" × 14½" sides and 2 on 22" × 8" sides.

STRATEGIES:

_____
_____
_____
_____
_____
_____

DEVELOPMENT:

_____
_____
_____
_____
_____
_____

VARIATIONS:

_____
_____
_____
_____
_____
_____

Tearing and Cutting

DEVELOPMENTAL LEVELS: 3–7 Years

AREAS OF DEVELOPMENT: Cognitive, Physical

BENEFITS TO CHILD: Eye-hand coordination; fine motor development; creativity; visual discrimination

MATERIALS:

- Scrap paper
- Strips of heavy paper (various widths from 1" to 3" and approximately 6" long)
- Pieces of plain heavy paper (4½" × 6")
- Scissors

HOW TO MAKE:

- ✂ Collect materials.

Tearing and Cutting

STRATEGIES:

_____
_____
_____
_____
_____
_____
_____
_____
_____
_____
_____

DEVELOPMENT:

_____
_____
_____
_____
_____
_____
_____
_____
_____
_____
_____

VARIATIONS:

_____
_____
_____
_____
_____
_____
_____
_____
_____
_____
_____

Easel in a Pizza Box

DEVELOPMENTAL LEVELS: 3–7 Years

AREAS OF DEVELOPMENT: Cognitive, Physical

BENEFITS TO CHILD: Eye-hand coordination; fine motor development; creativity; sensory experience

MATERIALS:

- Pizza box (17″ × 17″)
- 2 wood spring-clip clothespins
- Corrugated cardboard (15″ × 15″)
- 48″ duct tape
- White tagboard (15″ × 15″)
- White paper
- Markers
- Dustless chalk
- Pencils

HOW TO MAKE:

- ✂ Attach corrugated cardboard to inside of pizza box lid with duct tape.
- ✂ Attach paper to white tagboard using clothespins.

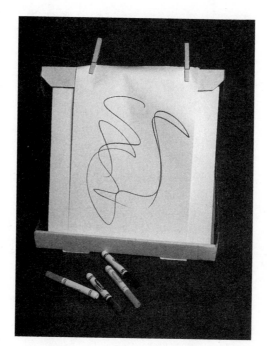

Easel in a Pizza Box

STRATEGIES:

_____
_____
_____
_____
_____
_____
_____
_____
_____
_____

DEVELOPMENT:

_____
_____
_____
_____
_____
_____
_____
_____
_____
_____

VARIATIONS:

_____
_____
_____
_____
_____
_____
_____
_____
_____
_____

Lots of Bubbles

DEVELOPMENTAL LEVELS: 3–7 Years

AREAS OF DEVELOPMENT: Cognitive, Physical, Social

BENEFITS TO CHILD: Sensory experience; cooperative play; fine and gross motor development

MATERIALS:

- Recipe for bubble mix
    - 3 cups liquid dishwashing detergent (e.g., Dawn) or baby shampoo
    - ½ cup glycerine
    - 2 gallons water
    - Mix together thoroughly.
- Nonbreakable dishpan
- Nonbreakable colander
- Berry baskets
- Plastic for needlepoint

- Nonbreakable shoe box (7" × 12¾")
- Paint mixers
- Rings
- Plastic pot scrubbers
- Bag for storage of materials
- Nonbreakable plastic items that allow bubble mix to flow through
- Gallon plastic containers with lids for storing bubble mix

Lots of Bubbles

HOW TO MAKE:

- ✂ Make bubble mix and store in gallon containers.
- ✂ Pour into dishpan or shoe box for use.

STRATEGIES:

_____

_____

_____

_____

_____

_____

_____

DEVELOPMENT:

_____

_____

_____

_____

_____

_____

_____

_____

_____

VARIATIONS:

_____

_____

_____

_____

_____

_____

_____

Block Cube Match

DEVELOPMENTAL LEVELS: 3–7 Years

AREAS OF DEVELOPMENT: Cognitive, Physical

BENEFITS TO CHILD: Mathematics concepts; visual discrimination; eye-hand coordination; emergent literacy

MATERIALS:

- 1" square blocks (6 brown, 12 black, 7 white)
- 4 poster boards (5" × 11")
- Clear self-adhesive plastic or laminate
- Permanent markers (black, red)
- 1¾" peel-and-stick plastic numbers (4, 6, 7, 8)
- Basket or box for storage

HOW TO MAKE:

- On each card (4, 6, 7, 8), write number word, attach number and draw outline in red for appropriate number of cubes.
- Cover cards on both sides with clear self-adhesive plastic or laminate.

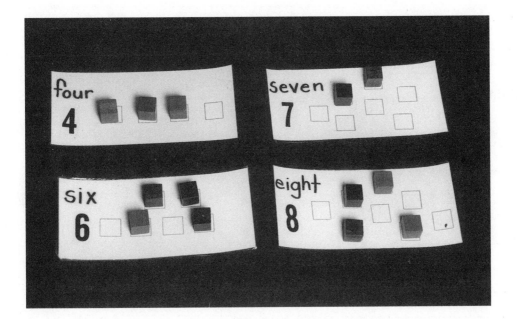

Block Cube Match

STRATEGIES:

_____
_____
_____
_____
_____
_____
_____
_____

DEVELOPMENT:

_____
_____
_____
_____
_____
_____
_____
_____
_____

VARIATIONS:

_____
_____
_____
_____
_____
_____
_____
_____
_____

Chalkboard in a Box

DEVELOPMENTAL LEVELS: 3–7 Years

AREAS OF DEVELOPMENT: Cognitive, Physical

BENEFITS TO CHILD: Eye-hand coordination; fine motor development; color concepts; creativity

MATERIALS:

- Pizza box (13" square)
- Chalkboard paint
- Eraser
- Dustless nontoxic chalk (white and colors)

HOW TO MAKE:

- Paint all inside surfaces of pizza box with nontoxic chalkboard paint (3 to 4 coats), letting dry 12 hours between coats.
- Place chalk and eraser inside box.

Chalkboard in a Box

STRATEGIES:

_____
_____
_____
_____
_____
_____
_____
_____
_____
_____

DEVELOPMENT:

_____
_____
_____
_____
_____
_____
_____
_____
_____
_____

VARIATIONS:

_____
_____
_____
_____
_____
_____
_____
_____
_____
_____
_____

Writing on Plexiglas

DEVELOPMENTAL LEVELS: 3–7 Years

AREAS OF DEVELOPMENT: Cognitive, Physical, Social

BENEFITS TO CHILD: Eye-hand coordination; fine motor development; creativity; cooperative play; sensory experience

MATERIALS:

- Plexiglas (30" × 30")
- Erasable nontoxic markers
- Finger paint
- Shaving cream
- Tempra paint
- 120" duct tape
- Lines, letters, numbers, shapes on cards (See Match, Copy, Write activity in 4–7 Years section.)

HOW TO MAKE:

- ✂ Put duct tape around the four edges of the Plexiglas.
- ✂ Put cards under Plexiglas.

Writing on Plexiglas

STRATEGIES:

_____
_____
_____
_____
_____
_____
_____
_____
_____

DEVELOPMENT:

_____
_____
_____
_____
_____
_____
_____
_____
_____
_____
_____

VARIATIONS:

_____
_____
_____
_____
_____
_____
_____
_____
_____
_____
_____
_____

Pat, Shake, and Dance

DEVELOPMENTAL LEVELS: 3–7 Years

AREAS OF DEVELOPMENT: Cognitive, Emotional, Physical, Social

BENEFITS TO CHILD: Creativity; express feelings; sensory discrimination; cooperative play; language development

MATERIALS:

- 5½" round container with lid
- Sand, buttons, rice, and so forth (variety for different sounds)
- Surveyor's tape or ribbon (variety of colors)
- Hot glue gun and glue sticks
- Tape

HOW TO MAKE:

- Place "sound" material in container.
- Attach streamers to inside edge with tape.
- Attach several pieces of surveyor's tape to inside edge of container with tape, approximately 12" to 14" pieces.
- Attach lid with hot glue.

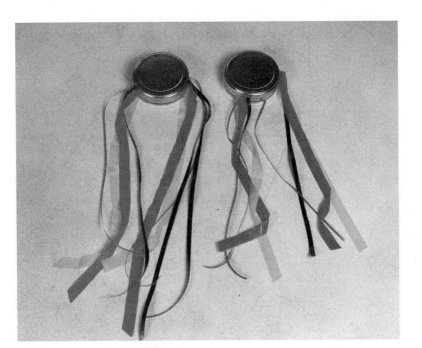

Pat, Shake, and Dance

STRATEGIES:

_____
_____
_____
_____
_____
_____
_____
_____
_____

DEVELOPMENT:

_____
_____
_____
_____
_____
_____
_____
_____
_____
_____
_____

VARIATIONS:

_____
_____
_____
_____
_____
_____
_____
_____
_____
_____
_____
_____
_____

Matching and Marking

DEVELOPMENTAL LEVELS: 3–7 Years

AREAS OF DEVELOPMENT: Cognitive, Physical

BENEFITS TO CHILD: Eye-hand coordination; fine motor development; size and shape concept development; matching; visual discrimination

MATERIALS:

- 5 pieces white tagboard (6" × 11")
- 26 pieces white tagboard (5" × 6")
- 20 pieces two colors of construction paper (6" × 9")
- Wipe off, nontoxic crayons
- Clear self-adhesive plastic or laminate (12" × 400")
- Permanent black marker
- 4" black letters of alphabet
- Eraser
- Ruler

Matching and Marking

HOW TO MAKE:

- ✂ Make 2 or 3 lines (curved, straight, angles) on each 6″ × 11″ piece of tagboard.

- ✂ Attach letters of alphabet to 5″ × 6″ tagboard pieces.

- ✂ Make sets of shapes, lines, and so forth on 6″ × 9″ pieces of construction paper.

- ✂ Cover all pieces with clear self-adhesive plastic or laminate.

STRATEGIES:

DEVELOPMENT:

VARIATIONS:

Dinosaur Dig

DEVELOPMENTAL LEVELS: 3–7 Years

AREAS OF DEVELOPMENT: Cognitive, Emotional, Physical, Social

BENEFITS TO CHILD: Eye-hand coordination; visual discrimination; sensory experience; cooperative play

MATERIALS:

- Wallpaper wetting tray (8" × 33" × 4¼")
- Fabric bolt (32" × 7" × 1")
- Colored self-adhesive plastic or laminate (20" × 36")
- White Velcro (20" × ¾")
- Sand (3½" deep in tray)

- Dinosaurs in eggs (4 green, 3 yellow, 4 orange or red, 3 dark pink)
- 2 plastic refrigerator egg containers that each hold 7 eggs
- 2 metal or plastic ice cube tongs
- 2 small shovels

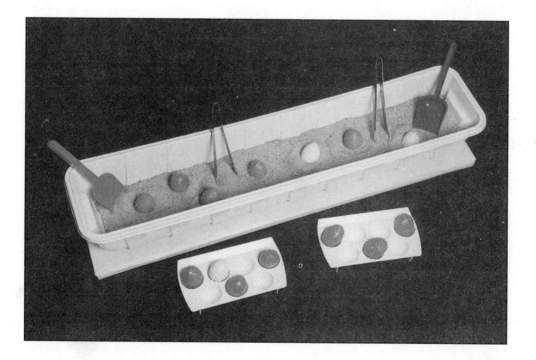

Dinosaur Dig

HOW TO MAKE:

- Cover fabric bolt with colored self-adhesive plastic.
- Attach Velcro, 5" pieces of hook and loop side on two ridges on bottom of wetting tray at each end.
- Place sand in tray.
- Bury eggs in sand.

STRATEGIES:

_____
_____
_____
_____
_____
_____
_____
_____

DEVELOPMENT:

_____
_____
_____
_____
_____
_____
_____

VARIATIONS:

_____
_____
_____
_____
_____
_____
_____
_____
_____

Apple Tree

DEVELOPMENTAL LEVELS: 3–7 Years

AREAS OF DEVELOPMENT: Cognitive, Physical, Social

BENEFITS TO CHILD: Mathematics concepts; emergent literacy; cooperative play

MATERIALS:

- Brown butcher paper (21" × 28")
- Green butcher paper (27" × 32")
- Manila folder or tagboard (12" × 18")
- Red tagboard (18" × 24")
- Clear self-adhesive plastic or laminate (33" × 133")
- 10" sticky-back Velcro
- Black permanent marker

Apple Tree

HOW TO MAKE:

✁ Open manila folder and write inside:

> Ten red apples growing on a tree,
> Five for you and five for me.
> Help me shake the tree just so,
> And ten red apples fall down
> below.

✁ Cut out 10 apples from red tagboard and write a number word from one to ten on each.

✁ Cut out tree trunk from brown butcher paper.

✁ Cut out tree foliage from green butcher paper.

✁ With clear self-adhesive plastic or laminate cover manila folder, tree trunk, tree foliage, and apples.

✁ Attach 1" piece of loop side of Velcro to each apple.

✁ Attach 1" piece of hook side of Velcro in scattered places on tree foliage.

STRATEGIES:

_____
_____
_____
_____
_____

DEVELOPMENT:

_____
_____
_____
_____
_____

VARIATIONS:

_____
_____
_____
_____
_____

Growing from Seeds

DEVELOPMENTAL LEVELS: 3–7 Years

AREAS OF DEVELOPMENT: Cognitive, Physical, Social

BENEFITS TO CHILD: Sensory experience; science/nature; observation; cause and effect; mathematics concepts; cooperative play; eye-hand coordination

MATERIALS:

- Plastic container with lid or cover (14" × 17" × 6½")
- Potting soil
- Plastic bucket (2 or 3 lb margarine tub)
- Seeds: pumpkin, radish, wild-flower
- 2 plastic shovels
- 2 plastic scoops
- Green tagboard (9" × 12")
- Pink tagboard (12" × 36")

- Black marker
- Black self-adhesive numbers (1 to 10)
- 20 tongue depressors
- Clear self-adhesive plastic or laminate (12" × 90")
- 2 pair gardening gloves
- Plastic or fabric bag for storage
- 4" square self-adhesive plastic pieces (pink, blue, green, brown, red, white)

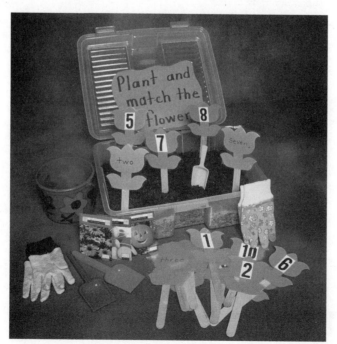

Growing from Seeds

HOW TO MAKE:

- Place potting soil in plastic container for planting seeds.
- Write "Plant and match the flowers." on green tagboard.
- Cut flowers from pink tagboard.
- Cover green and pink tagboard items with clear self-adhesive plastic or laminate.
- Attach a tongue depressor to each flower.
- Cut flowers and leaves from colored self-adhesive plastic and attach to plastic bucket.

STRATEGIES:

_____

_____

_____

_____

_____

_____

_____

_____

DEVELOPMENT:

_____

_____

_____

_____

_____

_____

_____

VARIATIONS:

_____

_____

_____

_____

_____

_____

_____

_____

Big and Little Red Cars

DEVELOPMENTAL LEVELS: 3–7 Years

AREAS OF DEVELOPMENT: Cognitive, Physical

BENEFITS TO CHILD: Mathematics concepts; following directions

MATERIALS:

- ⊕ Yellow tagboard (18" × 18")
- ⊕ Red permanent marker
- ⊕ 2 shower curtain hooks
- ⊕ Red tagboard (12" × 36")
- ⊕ Clear self-adhesive plastic or laminate (64" × 36")
- ⊕ Hole punch
- ⊕ Scissors

Big and Little Red Cars

HOW TO MAKE:

- Cut 2 irregular pieces approximately 10" × 20" from yellow tagboard.
- Print "How many *little* red cars can you count?" on one piece.
- Print "How many *big* red cars can you count?" on the other piece.
- Cut out 15 big cars or obtain ready-made cars.
- Cut out 20 little cars or obtain ready-made cars.
- Cover yellow tagboard pieces with clear self-adhesive plastic or laminate.
- Punch holes in car windows.
- Punch hole in yellow tagboard pieces.
- Using shower curtain hooks, attach little and big cars to appropriate yellow tagboard pieces.

STRATEGIES:

DEVELOPMENT:

VARIATIONS:

Bugs, Bugs, Bugs

DEVELOPMENTAL LEVELS: 3–7 Years

AREAS OF DEVELOPMENT: Cognitive, Physical, Social

BENEFITS TO CHILD: Eye-hand coordination; observation skills; cooperative play; language development

MATERIALS:

- 11 yellow tagboard 4'' circles
- 3 red tagboard 4'' circles
- 4 blue tagboard 4'' circles
- Pictures or stickers: bumblebee, spider, cockroach, centipede, scorpion, praying mantis, ladybug, carpenter ant, firefly
- Permanent black marker
- Clear self-adhesive plastic or laminate (9'' × 80'')
- Apron with 9 pockets (purchase or make)
- 9'' Velcro
- Book about insects (purchase or make)

Bugs, Bugs, Bugs

HOW TO MAKE:

- ✄ Sew 1" pieces of loop side of Velcro to middle of each pocket on apron.

- ✄ Attach insect pictures in center of 9 circles.

- ✄ Write an insect name on each of the other 9 circles with black marker.

- ✄ Cover front and back circles with clear self-adhesive plastic or laminate.

- ✄ Attach 1" piece of hook side of Velcro to back of circles that have words on them.

STRATEGIES:

_____
_____
_____
_____
_____
_____
_____
_____

DEVELOPMENT:

_____
_____
_____
_____
_____
_____
_____
_____
_____

VARIATIONS:

_____
_____
_____
_____
_____
_____
_____
_____

Five Speckled Frogs

DEVELOPMENTAL LEVELS: 3–7 Years

AREAS OF DEVELOPMENT: Cognitive, Physical, Social

BENEFITS TO CHILD: Eye-hand coordination; fine motor development; cooperative play; language development

MATERIALS:

- Pizza box (14" square)
- 12" clear plastic plant saucer
- 5 speckled frogs
- 11" empty paper towel cylinder
- Newspaper
- 3" Velcro
- White tape (1" × 52")
- Black permanent marker
- Wood-grain self-adhesive plastic (8" × 12")
- 5 self-adhesive bug stickers (ladybugs, spiders, and/or grasshoppers)
- White tagboard (13" × 13")
- Clear self-adhesive plastic or laminate (14" × 28")

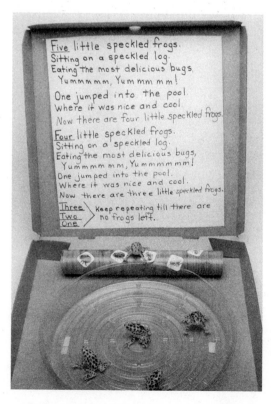

Five Speckled Frogs

HOW TO MAKE:

- Write poem "Five Little Speckled Frogs" on tagboard.
- Cover with clear self-adhesive plastic or laminate.
- Stuff towel cylinder with newspaper and cover with wood-grain self-adhesive plastic.
- Attach 5 bugs to cylinder.
- Attach loop side of 1'' Velcro pieces 2'' from end of cylinder.
- Attach hook side of 1'' Velcro pieces inside bottom of pizza box near top edge.
- Attach loop side of ½'' Velcro to bottom of plant saucer, 1'' from opposite edges.
- Attach hook side of ½'' Velcro pieces inside bottom of pizza box to center plant saucer.

STRATEGIES:

_____
_____
_____
_____
_____
_____
_____
_____

DEVELOPMENT:

_____
_____
_____
_____
_____
_____
_____
_____

VARIATIONS:

_____
_____
_____
_____
_____
_____

There Was a Little Turtle

DEVELOPMENTAL LEVELS: 3–8 Years

AREAS OF DEVELOPMENT: Cognitive, Emotional, Physical

BENEFITS TO CHILD: Creativity; language development; self-concept development

MATERIALS:

- Cardboard box (9" × 10" × 14")
- Colored self-adhesive plastic or laminate (36" × 40")
- Turtle cap (purchase)
- Turtle puppet (purchase)
- Blue felt or heavy fabric (12" × 15")
- Poem

    There was a little turtle
    Who lived in a box
    S/he swam in a puddle
    S/he climbed on a rock
    S/he snapped at a minnow
    S/he snapped at a flea
    S/he snapped at a mosquito
    S/he snapped at me
    S/he caught the minnow
    S/he caught the flea
    S/he caught the mosquito
    But she didn't catch me!

- Pictures of flea, mosquito, and minnow
- 3 pieces black tagboard (9" × 12")
- Clear self-adhesive plastic or laminate (13" × 60")
- Rubber cement
- Rock with bag for storage

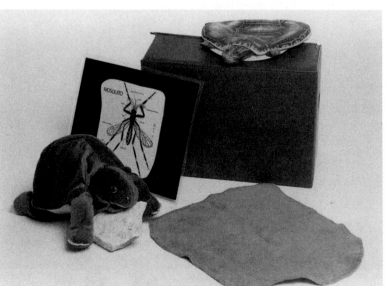

3–8 Years ✂ **193**

There Was a Little Turtle

HOW TO MAKE:

- Cover cardboard box with self-adhesive plastic or laminate.

- Attach pictures of mosquito, flea, and minnow to tagboard with rubber cement.

- Cover tagboard pictures with clear self-adhesive plastic or laminate.

- Cut irregular shaped pond from felt or fabric and hem.

STRATEGIES:

_____
_____
_____
_____
_____
_____
_____
_____

DEVELOPMENT:

_____
_____
_____
_____
_____
_____
_____
_____

VARIATIONS:

_____
_____
_____
_____
_____
_____
_____
_____

Magnet Tube

DEVELOPMENTAL LEVELS: 3–8 Years

AREAS OF DEVELOPMENT: Cognitive, Physical

BENEFITS TO CHILD: Creativity; curiosity; eye-hand coordination; sensory experience; cooperative play

MATERIALS:

- Fabric bolt (7½'' × 30'')
- Colored self-adhesive plastic or laminate
- Florescent tube lamp shadow cover with 2 caps
- Three 1¼'' Velcro pieces
- Magnet wand
- 150 colored paper clips
- Four 1¼'' pieces electrical tape
- Hot glue gun and glue sticks

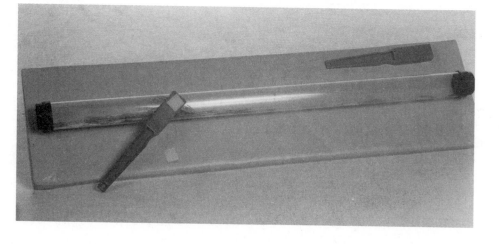

Magnet Tube

HOW TO MAKE:

✄ Cover fabric bolt with colored self-adhesive plastic.

✄ Cover holes in caps on ends of tube guard with electrical tape, one piece on inside and one on outside of cap.

✄ Place paper clips inside tube.

✄ Attach caps to tube with hot glue.

✄ Attach loop side of Velcro to tube caps and hook side of Velcro to fabric bolt approximately 1" from each end so they meet.

✄ Attach loop side of Velcro to side of magnetic wand and hook side on fabric bolt near side, approximately 9" from end.

STRATEGIES:

_____
_____
_____
_____
_____
_____
_____

DEVELOPMENT:

_____
_____
_____
_____
_____
_____
_____

VARIATIONS:

_____
_____
_____
_____
_____
_____
_____
_____

Cork Prints

DEVELOPMENTAL LEVELS: 4–5 Years

AREAS OF DEVELOPMENT: Cognitive, Physical

BENEFITS TO CHILD: Size and shape concepts; eye-hand coordination; fine motor development; sequencing

MATERIALS:

- Purchase nontoxic stamp pad or use tempra paint on sponge in margarine tub or meat tray
- Corks (2¼", 1½", 1¼", ⅞", ¾", ½" diameters)
- Unbreakable storage container
- Adding machine paper

HOW TO MAKE:

- ✂ If making stamp pad, saturate sponge with liquid tempra paint.
- ✂ Purchase or collect items.

Cork Prints

STRATEGIES:

_____
_____
_____
_____
_____
_____
_____
_____
_____
_____

DEVELOPMENT:

_____
_____
_____
_____
_____
_____
_____
_____
_____
_____

VARIATIONS:

_____
_____
_____
_____
_____
_____
_____
_____
_____
_____
_____

Help Me Find My Carrot

DEVELOPMENTAL LEVELS: 4–5 Years

AREAS OF DEVELOPMENT: Cognitive, Physical

BENEFITS TO CHILD: Mathematics concepts; language development, emergent literacy; eye-hand coordination

MATERIALS:

- 6 orange carrots with green tops (2½" × 8")
- 6 white rabbits (7" × 10")
- Twenty-one ¾" black self-adhesive dots
- Black permanent marker
- Green poster board (8½" × 11")
- Clear self-adhesive plastic or laminate (12" × 146")

Help Me Find My Carrot

HOW TO MAKE:

- ✄ Carrots with ⅜'' white circles (1, 2, 3, 4, 5, 6) (make or purchase).

- ✄ Attach black self-adhesive dots to rabbits (1 to 6).

- ✄ Write number words on each rabbit.

- ✄ Write "Help me find my carrot" on green poster board.

- ✄ Cover all on both sides with clear self-adhesive plastic or laminate.

STRATEGIES:

_____
_____
_____
_____
_____
_____
_____
_____

DEVELOPMENT:

_____
_____
_____
_____
_____
_____
_____
_____

VARIATIONS:

_____
_____
_____
_____
_____
_____
_____

Sequencing

DEVELOPMENTAL LEVELS: 4–5 Years

AREAS OF DEVELOPMENT: Cognitive, Physical, Social

BENEFITS TO CHILD: Language development; visual discrimination; sequencing; cooperative play

MATERIALS:

- Fabric bolt (8" × 23")
- Colored self-adhesive plastic or laminate (22" × 23")
- 8" Velcro
- Sequence pictures—2 sets with 4 in each series (purchase or draw)
- Clear self-adhesive plastic or laminate (8" × 32")
- Rubber cement
- Sequencing (written on 1¼" × 6½" card)

Sequencing

HOW TO MAKE:

- ✄ Cover fabric bolt with colored self-adhesive plastic or laminate.

- ✄ Cover front and back of pictures with clear self-adhesive plastic or laminate.

- ✄ Cut Velcro into 1" pieces.

- ✄ Attach 4 Velcro pieces to covered fabric bolt in middle of bolt, 5" from top and 4" apart.

- ✄ Attach "Sequencing" word card to top of covered fabric bolt.

- ✄ Attach Velcro to back of pictures.

STRATEGIES:

_____
_____
_____
_____
_____
_____
_____
_____

DEVELOPMENT:

_____
_____
_____
_____
_____
_____
_____
_____

VARIATIONS:

_____
_____
_____
_____
_____
_____
_____

Pom-pom Tray

DEVELOPMENTAL LEVELS: 4–6 Years

AREAS OF DEVELOPMENT: Cognitive, Physical

BENEFITS TO CHILD: Eye-hand coordination; creativity; fine motor development; visual discrimination

MATERIALS:

- Ice cube tray (one that makes 90 ½'' cubes)
- 90 pom-pom balls (½'' diameter)
- Strawberry huller
- Ziploc bag for pom-pom ball storage

HOW TO MAKE:

- ✄ Collect materials.

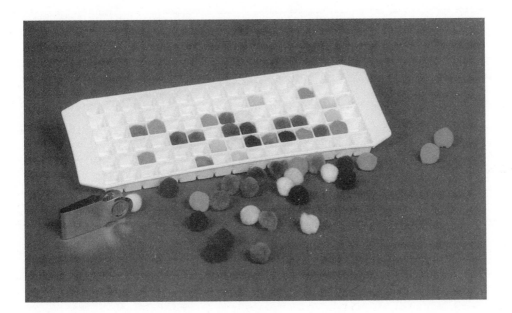

Pom-pom Tray

STRATEGIES:

_____
_____
_____
_____
_____
_____
_____
_____
_____
_____

DEVELOPMENT:

_____
_____
_____
_____
_____
_____
_____
_____
_____
_____
_____

VARIATIONS:

_____
_____
_____
_____
_____
_____
_____
_____
_____
_____

Writing on Styrofoam

DEVELOPMENTAL LEVELS: 4–6 Years

AREAS OF DEVELOPMENT: Cognitive, Emotional, Physical, Social

BENEFITS TO CHILD: Eye-hand coordination; fine motor development; creativity; sensory experience

MATERIALS:

- 75 to 100 golf tees
- Plastic container for storing golf tees (1 lb margarine tub or similar size)
- New styrofoam meat trays (variety of sizes)
- Styrofoam plates

HOW TO MAKE:

- Collect materials.

Writing on Styrofoam

STRATEGIES:

_____

_____

_____

_____

_____

_____

_____

_____

_____

DEVELOPMENT:

_____

_____

_____

_____

_____

_____

_____

_____

_____

_____

_____

VARIATIONS:

_____

_____

_____

_____

_____

_____

_____

_____

_____

_____

_____

Button Count

DEVELOPMENTAL LEVELS: 4–6 Years

AREAS OF DEVELOPMENT: Cognitive, Physical

BENEFITS TO CHILD: Mathematics concepts; visual discrimination; eye-hand coordination

MATERIALS:

- 1 plastic lid (11½" diameter from 5-gallon container)
- 8 plastic lids (2½" diameter)
- 1 plastic cup (2½" × 1")
- Self-adhesive plastic numbers (1 to 8)
- Hot glue gun and glue sticks
- Clear nail polish
- 36 buttons (assorted sizes and colors)
- Ziploc bag for button storage

Button Count

HOW TO MAKE:

- ✄ With hot glue, attach small lids around inside edge of large lid.
- ✄ With hot glue, attach cup in center of large lid.
- ✄ Place plastic numbers on small lids and cover with clear nail polish.

STRATEGIES:

_____
_____
_____
_____
_____
_____
_____
_____

DEVELOPMENT:

_____
_____
_____
_____
_____
_____
_____
_____
_____

VARIATIONS:

_____
_____
_____
_____
_____
_____
_____

Picture Match

DEVELOPMENTAL LEVELS: 4–6 Years

AREAS OF DEVELOPMENT: Cognitive, Physical

BENEFITS TO CHILD: Visual discrimination; eye-hand coordination; fine motor development; language development

MATERIALS:

- 22 plastic milk jug lids
- Ten ¾" self-adhesive dots (2 red, 2 green, 2 yellow, 2 orange, 2 hot pink)
- 12 animal pictures—2 pigs, 2 turtles, 2 seals, 2 hens, 2 apples, 2 circles (purchased or cut from magazines, catalogs, and for forth)
- Glue
- Disinfectant (1 tablespoon chlorine bleach in 1 quart water)
- Plastic or fabric bag

Picture Match

HOW TO MAKE:

✄ Wash and disinfect milk jug lids.　　✄ Attach pictures to lids.

STRATEGIES:

_____

_____

_____

_____

_____

_____

_____

_____

DEVELOPMENT:

_____

_____

_____

_____

_____

_____

_____

_____

_____

VARIATIONS:

_____

_____

_____

_____

_____

_____

_____

_____

_____

_____

Spools and Knobs

DEVELOPMENTAL LEVELS: 4–6 Years

AREAS OF DEVELOPMENT: Cognitive, Physical, Social

BENEFITS TO CHILD: Mathematics concepts; eye-hand coordination; fine motor development; cooperative play

MATERIALS:

- Box (7" × 9" × 2¾")
- Black and white check self-adhesive plastic (9" × 26")
- 8 pieces poster board (one 3" × 6"; seven 5" × 8")
- Clear plastic self-adhesive envelope (4" × 6½")
- Forty-four ¾" self-adhesive black dots
- Large black permanent marker
- 48 wooden items (spools, knobs, disks, and so forth)
- Clear self-adhesive plastic or laminate (8" × 85")

Age Level (Years)

2
3
4
5
6
7
8

Spools and Knobs

HOW TO MAKE:

- ✂ Cover box with black and white check self-adhesive plastic.

- ✂ Attach clear plastic self-adhesive envelope to outside top of box.

- ✂ Attach black dots and write numbers and number words on 5" × 8" poster boards (2, 3, 4, 5, 6, 9, 10)

- ✂ Write "How Many?" on 3" × 6" poster boards.

- ✂ Cover all cards with clear self-adhesive plastic or laminate.

STRATEGIES:

_____

_____

_____

_____

_____

_____

_____

_____

DEVELOPMENT:

_____

_____

_____

_____

_____

_____

_____

VARIATIONS:

_____

_____

_____

_____

_____

_____

_____

Primary Colors

DEVELOPMENTAL LEVELS: 4–6 Years

AREAS OF DEVELOPMENT: Cognitive, Physical

BENEFITS TO CHILD: Eye-hand coordination; emergent literacy; language development; cooperative play

MATERIALS:

- Plastic travel soap containers (3½" × 4½"; 1 blue, 1 yellow, 1 red)
- 3" Velcro
- 3 pieces poster board (2¼" × 4", 2¼" × 4½", 2¼" × 6¼")
- Small items to match colors of containers (e.g., bears, beads, numbers, sticks, cars, and so forth)
- Clear self-adhesive plastic or laminate

Primary Colors

HOW TO MAKE:

- ✂ Write color words on poster board cards, red on 2¼" × 4", blue on 2¼" × 4½", and yellow on 2¼" × 6¼"). Color words may be purchased.

- ✂ Cover poster board word cards with clear self-adhesive plastic.

- ✂ Attach Velcro to back of each word card.

- ✂ Attach Velcro to top of each soap container.

- ✂ Place appropriate small items in each color container.

STRATEGIES:

DEVELOPMENT:

VARIATIONS:

How Many Animals

DEVELOPMENTAL LEVELS: 4–6 Years

AREAS OF DEVELOPMENT: Cognitive, Physical

BENEFITS TO CHILD: Mathematics concepts; eye-hand coordination; fine motor development; visual discrimination

MATERIALS:

- Box (12" × 18" × 2½") with 8 sections
- Primary color self-adhesive plastic or laminate (20" × 36")
- Scissors
- 5" self-adhesive numbers (1 to 8)
- Variety of small animals: 1 goose, 2 chickens, 3 cows, 4 geese, 5 dogs, 6 cows, 7 ponies, 8 pigs
- Storage bag for animals

How Many Animals

HOW TO MAKE:

- ✂ Cover outside of box with self-adhesive plastic or laminate.
- ✂ Place self-adhesive numbers inside box sections.
- ✂ Store animals in bag.

STRATEGIES:

_____
_____
_____
_____
_____
_____
_____
_____
_____

DEVELOPMENT:

_____
_____
_____
_____
_____
_____
_____
_____
_____
_____

VARIATIONS:

_____
_____
_____
_____
_____
_____
_____
_____

Stack the Washers

DEVELOPMENTAL LEVELS: 4–6 Years

AREAS OF DEVELOPMENT: Cognitive, Physical, Social

BENEFITS TO CHILD: Eye-hand coordination; sensory experience; mathematics concepts — counting; cooperative play

MATERIALS:

- Fabric bolt
- Colored self-adhesive plastic (18" × 28")
- 7" sticky-back Velcro
- 2 room deodorizer containers
- 40 water hose washers

HOW TO MAKE:

- Cover fabric bolt with self-adhesive plastic.
- Cut sticky-back Velcro into 4 pieces. Attach Velcro to room deodorizer containers, 2 pieces of one side of Velcro to bottom of each.
- Attach other side of Velcro to fabric bolt, approximately 8" from each end and matching Velcro on bottom of room deodorizer containers.

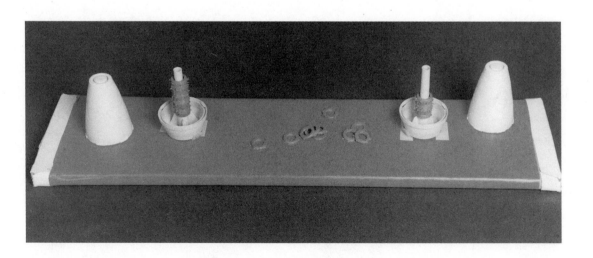

Stack the Washers

STRATEGIES:

_____
_____
_____
_____
_____
_____
_____
_____
_____
_____

DEVELOPMENT:

_____
_____
_____
_____
_____
_____
_____
_____
_____
_____
_____
_____

VARIATIONS:

_____
_____
_____
_____
_____
_____
_____
_____
_____
_____
_____
_____
_____

Marble Match

DEVELOPMENTAL LEVELS: 4–6 Years

AREAS OF DEVELOPMENT: Cognitive, Physical, Social

BENEFITS TO CHILD: Cooperative play; eye-hand coordination; mathematics concepts — one-to-one correspondence; fine motor skills; sensory experience

MATERIALS:

- Fabric bolt
- Self-adhesive plastic or laminate (18" × 28")
- 2 margarine containers with lids
- Bath mat with small suction circles (two 6" × 7" pieces)
- 84 marbles
- Hot glue gun and glue sticks

HOW TO MAKE:

- Cover bolt with self-adhesive plastic or laminate.
- With hot glue, attach margarine containers, one near the end and the other near the middle of bolt.
- With hot glue, attach bath mat pieces, one near the end and the other between margarine containers.

Marble Match

STRATEGIES:

_____
_____
_____
_____
_____
_____
_____
_____
_____
_____
_____

DEVELOPMENT:

_____
_____
_____
_____
_____
_____
_____
_____
_____
_____
_____

VARIATIONS:

_____
_____
_____
_____
_____
_____
_____
_____
_____
_____
_____
_____

Catch and Count the Dots

DEVELOPMENTAL LEVELS: 4–6 Years

AREAS OF DEVELOPMENT: Cognitive, Physical, Social

BENEFITS TO CHILD: Eye-hand coordination; recognizing and naming colors; cause and effect of magnets; mathematics concepts; cooperative play

MATERIALS:

- 9" × 12" tagboard
- 13" × 20" clear self-adhesive plastic or laminate
- Wide black marker
- Baby food lids
- 1¼" self-adhesive dots—46 yellow, 28 red, 11 blue
- 2 magnet wands
- Box lid (20" × 23")
- Plastic or fabric storage bag
- 60" duct tape

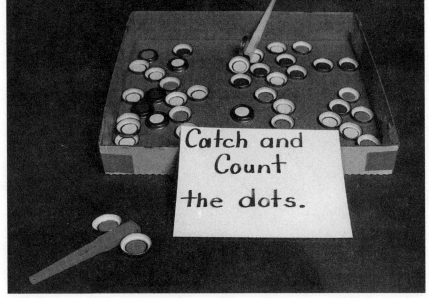

4–6 Years ✂ **223**

Catch and Count the Dots

HOW TO MAKE:

- ✂ Write "Catch and Count the Dots." on tagboard and cover with clear self-adhesive plastic or laminate.

- ✂ Place self-adhesive dots on lids, one inside and one outside of same color.

- ✂ Reinforce corners of box lid with duct tape.

STRATEGIES:

_____

_____

_____

_____

_____

_____

_____

_____

_____

DEVELOPMENT:

_____

_____

_____

_____

_____

_____

_____

_____

_____

VARIATIONS:

_____

_____

_____

_____

_____

_____

_____

_____

_____

Five and Nine

DEVELOPMENTAL LEVELS: 4–6 Years

AREAS OF DEVELOPMENT: Cognitive, Physical, Social

BENEFITS TO CHILD: Visual discrimination; mathematics concepts; sensory experience; cooperative play

MATERIALS:

- Poster board (green 9" × 10", blue 9" × 10")
- Clear self-adhesive plastic or laminate (10" × 36")
- Nine 1¾" white paper circles
- Five 2¾" circles—red, purple, blue, orange, yellow (purchased or made from construction paper)
- Words "five" and "nine" (made or purchased)
- 5 bottle tops from juice or milk containers (orange, yellow, blue, purple, red)
- 9 blue poker chips
- Fourteen ½" Velcro pieces

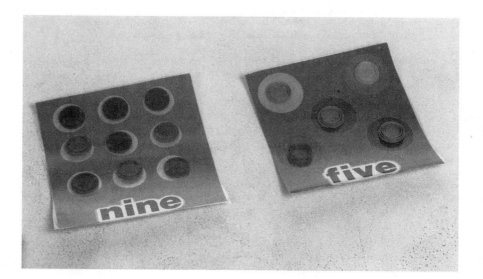

Five and Nine

HOW TO MAKE:

- ✄ Attach "nine" to blue poster board at bottom.
- ✄ Attach 9 white circles to blue poster board card, 3 rows of 3 approximately ½" apart.
- ✄ Attach 5 color circles to green poster board card with approximately 1" between circles.
- ✄ Attach "five" to green poster board card at bottom.
- ✄ Cover green and blue poster board cards with clear self-adhesive plastic or laminate.
- ✄ Attach hook pieces of Velcro to all circles on green and blue poster board cards.
- ✄ Attach loop side pieces of Velcro to poker chips and bottle tops.

STRATEGIES:

DEVELOPMENT:

VARIATIONS:

Reach and Count

DEVELOPMENTAL LEVELS: 4–6 Years

AREAS OF DEVELOPMENT: Cognitive, Physical

BENEFITS TO CHILD: Fine motor development; mathematics concepts; language development; visual discrimination

MATERIALS:

- 12 canning lids (2⅝" diameter)
- 12" magnetic tape
- 1" self-adhesive numbers (1 to 12)
- Six 5" black vinyl spiders with suction cups
- Six 6" black vinyl lizards with suction cups

- Box (9" × 10" × 4¾")
- Colored self-adhesive plastic or laminate (10" × 32")
- Large black permanent marker
- Hot glue gun and glue sticks
- Metal stove protector (14" × 17")

Reach and Count

HOW TO MAKE:

- ✂ Cover box with colored self-adhesive plastic.

- ✂ Write "Reach and Count" on one 9" × 10" side with permanent marker.

- ✂ Using hot glue, attach 1" piece of magnetic tape to inside of each canning lid.

- ✂ Cut oval opening (3½" × 6½") in top of box.

- ✂ Attach a self-adhesive number to each canning lid.

- ✂ Place lids, spiders, and lizards in box.

STRATEGIES:

DEVELOPMENT:

VARIATIONS:

Writing with Straws, Toothpicks, and Craft Sticks

DEVELOPMENTAL LEVELS: 4–7 Years

AREAS OF DEVELOPMENT: Cognitive, Physical

BENEFITS TO CHILD: Eye-hand coordination; fine motor development; creativity; sensory experience

MATERIALS:

- Tool tray (10" × 15")
- Variety of tagboard, cardboard, folders, and so forth (9" × 12")
- Box of colored tooth picks
- Craft or popsicle sticks— 200 colored, 200 natural wood
- 200 plastic drinking straws— assorted colors
- School glue or homemade paste (See recipe on Resource Information page in the Appendix.)

HOW TO MAKE:

- ✂ Collect materials.

Writing with Straws, Toothpicks, and Craft Sticks

STRATEGIES:

_____

_____

_____

_____

_____

_____

_____

_____

DEVELOPMENT:

_____

_____

_____

_____

_____

_____

_____

_____

_____

_____

VARIATIONS:

_____

_____

_____

_____

_____

_____

_____

_____

Sand Writing

DEVELOPMENTAL LEVELS: 4–7 Years

AREAS OF DEVELOPMENT: Cognitive, Physical

BENEFITS TO CHILD: Eye-hand coordination; creativity; fine motor development; sensory experience; cause and effect; cooperative play

MATERIALS:

- ⊛ Clear plastic shoe box (6½" × 12")
- ⊛ 3 small margarine containers
- ⊛ Tagboard pieces (9" × 12")
- ⊛ 3 bottles of glue or homemade paste (See recipe on Resource Information page in the Appendix.)
- ⊛ 3 plastic spoons
- ⊛ 6 cups sand

HOW TO MAKE:

- ✀ Collect materials.

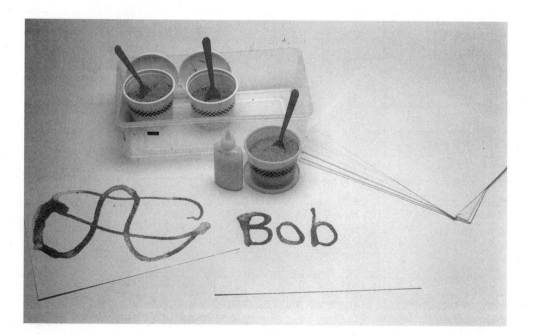

Sand Writing

STRATEGIES:

_____
_____
_____
_____
_____
_____
_____
_____
_____
_____
_____

DEVELOPMENT:

_____
_____
_____
_____
_____
_____
_____
_____
_____
_____
_____

VARIATIONS:

_____
_____
_____
_____
_____
_____
_____
_____
_____
_____
_____
_____

Vegetables

DEVELOPMENTAL LEVELS: 4–7 Years

AREAS OF DEVELOPMENT: Cognitive, Physical, Social

BENEFITS TO CHILD: Eye-hand coordination; fine motor development; concept development; learns health habits; language development; cultural awareness

MATERIALS:

- Plastic vegetables—corn, carrot, green pepper, lettuce, purple cabbage, tomato, red pepper, onion, zucchini, eggplant

- Basket to hold vegetables

- Flat box (9½" × 12" × 2½")

- Red self-adhesive plastic (12" × 36")

- 10 pieces clear plastic canvas (6½" × 10½")

- Black permanent markers

- 10 sheets paper (8½" × 11")

- Books about vegetables

Vegetables

HOW TO MAKE:

✂ Cover flat box with red self-adhesive plastic.

✂ In English or Spanish, write vegetable words on plastic canvas using black marker.

STRATEGIES:

_____
_____
_____
_____
_____
_____
_____
_____
_____

DEVELOPMENT:

_____
_____
_____
_____
_____
_____
_____
_____
_____

VARIATIONS:

_____
_____
_____
_____
_____
_____
_____
_____

Count the Beans

DEVELOPMENTAL LEVELS: 4–7 Years

AREAS OF DEVELOPMENT: Cognitive, Physical, Social

BENEFITS TO CHILD: Mathematics concepts; cooperative play; eye-hand coordination; fine motor development

MATERIALS:

- Pizza box (13" × 13")
- 12 unbreakable icing containers (2¼" diameter, 1" deep)
- ¾" black self-adhesive numbers (1 to 12)
- Clear nail polish
- Hot glue gun and glue sticks
- Purchase 78 red and white plastic beans (purchase)
- Bag or box for bean storage

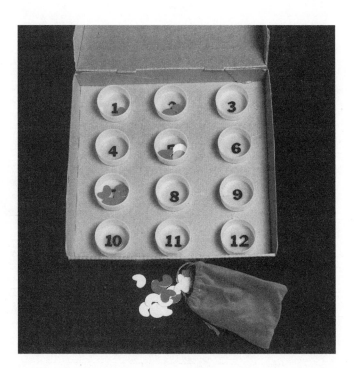

Count the Beans

HOW TO MAKE:

✂ With hot glue, attach icing containers in pizza box, 4 rows with 3 containers in each row.

✂ Stick numbers in containers and coat with several coats of clear nail polish.

STRATEGIES:

_____

_____

_____

_____

_____

_____

_____

_____

_____

DEVELOPMENT:

_____

_____

_____

_____

_____

_____

_____

_____

_____

VARIATIONS:

_____

_____

_____

_____

_____

_____

_____

_____

_____

Letter Match

DEVELOPMENTAL LEVELS: 4–7 Years

AREAS OF DEVELOPMENT: Cognitive, Physical

BENEFITS TO CHILD: Eye-hand coordination; visual discrimination; size and shape concept development; fine motor development

MATERIALS:

- 4 pieces tagboard (4½" × 5½")
- Black permanent markers
- Clear self-adhesive plastic or laminate (6" × 40")
- Erasable nontoxic crayons
- Eraser or piece of soft fabric

HOW TO MAKE:

- Make 4 cards with different letters as follows:

  Print 5 uppercase (capital) letters down left side of card and the same letters in lowercase (small) letters down right side of card in a different order.

- Cover cards with clear self-adhesive plastic or laminate.

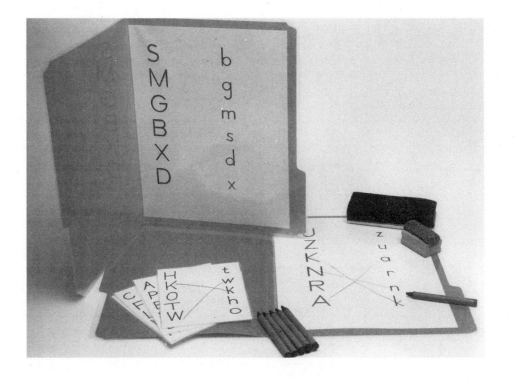

Letter Match

STRATEGIES:

_____
_____
_____
_____
_____
_____
_____
_____

DEVELOPMENT:

_____
_____
_____
_____
_____
_____
_____
_____
_____

VARIATIONS:

_____
_____
_____
_____
_____
_____
_____
_____
_____
_____
_____

Design Match

DEVELOPMENTAL LEVELS: 4–7 Years

AREAS OF DEVELOPMENT: Cognitive, Physical, Social

BENEFITS TO CHILD: Visual discrimination; eye-hand coordination; concept of shapes; cooperative play

MATERIALS:

- 5 sheets construction paper— 2 colors (9" × 12")
- Clear self-adhesive plastic or laminate (12" × 180")
- Black permanent marker
- Scissors
- Ruler

Design Match

HOW TO MAKE:

- ✂ Cut construction paper into twenty 6" × 9" pieces.
- ✂ Using markers, make pairs of designs, one on each color paper.
- ✂ Make the following pairs of designs:

  XX (two Xs or double X)

  _____ (horizontal line)

▭ (rectangle)

X (one X or single X)

☐ (square)

O (circle)

◇ (diamond)

/ (angled line)

△ (triangle)

⬡ (octagon)

STRATEGIES:

_____

_____

_____

_____

_____

_____

_____

DEVELOPMENT:

_____

_____

_____

_____

_____

_____

_____

VARIATIONS:

_____

_____

_____

_____

_____

_____

Big Puzzles

DEVELOPMENTAL LEVELS: 4–7 Years

AREAS OF DEVELOPMENT: Cognitive, Physical

BENEFITS TO CHILD: Context of shapes; fine motor development; language development

MATERIALS:

- Heavy plastic place mats with dinosaurs, animal designs, and so forth
- Scissors
- Permanent markers

HOW TO MAKE:

- Use scissors to cut place mat into 4 to 10 irregular pieces.
- Use markers to make identifying color or mark on back of each. (Suggest storing only two together.)
- Plastic or cloth storage bags.

Big Puzzles

STRATEGIES:

_____

_____

_____

_____

_____

_____

_____

_____

_____

DEVELOPMENT:

_____

_____

_____

_____

_____

_____

_____

_____

_____

_____

_____

VARIATIONS:

_____

_____

_____

_____

_____

_____

_____

_____

_____

_____

_____

_____

One to Twelve

DEVELOPMENTAL LEVELS: 4–7 Years

AREAS OF DEVELOPMENT: Cognitive, Physical, Social

BENEFITS TO CHILD: Cooperative play; mathematics concepts; visual discrimination; language development

MATERIALS:

- Variety of items such as:
  - 16 green bracelets
  - 16 bottle tops
  - 6 red bottle tops
  - 2 black wheels
  - 5 yellow bottle tops
  - 8 pigs
  - 3 orange bottle tops
  - 12 blue bottle tops
  - 9 white bottle tops
  - 9 purple bottle tops
  - 8 light blue ponies
- 3½" black self-adhesive numbers (1 to 12)
- Fabric or plastic bag for storing items (11" × 12")
- Clear plastic lingerie and stocking organizer (17" × 27")

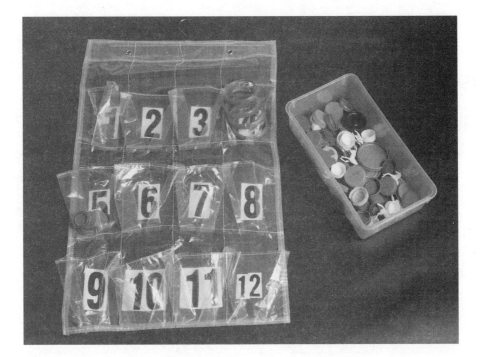

One to Twelve

HOW TO MAKE:

- ✀ Collect or ask parent to collect variety of bottle tops and other items.
- ✀ Store in bag.

- ✀ Purchase lingerie and stocking organizer.

STRATEGIES:

_____
_____
_____
_____
_____
_____
_____
_____

DEVELOPMENT:

_____
_____
_____
_____
_____
_____
_____
_____

VARIATIONS:

_____
_____
_____
_____
_____
_____
_____
_____

Number Count

DEVELOPMENTAL LEVELS: 4–7 Years

AREAS OF DEVELOPMENT: Cognitive, Physical

BENEFITS TO CHILD: Mathematics concepts; eye-hand coordination; fine motor development

MATERIALS:

- Fabric bolt
- Colored self-adhesive plastic (18" by 28")
- 10 sticky-back hooks
- 10 self-adhesive numbers (1 to 10)
- 55 plastic garbage ties

HOW TO MAKE:

- Cover fabric bolt with colored self-adhesive plastic.
- Attach hooks along one long side of fabric bolt.
- Place numbers 1 to 10 beside hooks.

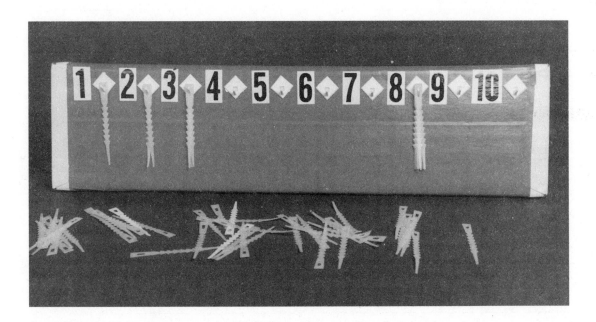

Number Count

STRATEGIES:

DEVELOPMENT:

VARIATIONS:

Match, Copy, Write

DEVELOPMENTAL LEVELS: 4–7 Years

AREAS OF DEVELOPMENT: Cognitive, Emotional, Social

BENEFITS TO CHILD: Eye-hand coordination; sensory experience; visual discrimination; cooperative play; fine motor development; observation skills

MATERIALS:

- 52 baby food jar lids
- White metal stove covers (14" × 17")
- White metal individual range burner covers (two 10" diameter; two 8" diameter; one 7" square)
- 26 uppercase and 26 lowercase self-adhesive ½" letters
- 52 magnets (1" diameter)
- Containers for storage of letters
- Nontoxic water base sealer

Match, Copy, Write

HOW TO MAKE:

✂ Wash lids in disinfectant (1 table-spoon chlorine bleach in 1 quart water) and dry completely.

✂ Attach a letter to inside of each lid.

✂ Cover each letter with sealer.

✂ Attach a magnet to outside of each lid.

STRATEGIES:

_____

_____

_____

_____

_____

_____

_____

DEVELOPMENT:

_____

_____

_____

_____

_____

_____

_____

_____

VARIATIONS:

_____

_____

_____

_____

_____

_____

_____

_____

Five, Ten, Fifteen

DEVELOPMENTAL LEVELS: 4–7 Years

AREAS OF DEVELOPMENT: Cognitive, Physical

BENEFITS TO CHILD: Mathematics concepts; language development; eye-hand coordination

MATERIALS:

- 3 plastic containers (½-half gallon with lids)
- 3" self-adhesive red numbers (two 1s, two 5s, one 0)
- Large black permanent marker
- 10 drink coasters (4" diameter)
- 15 aluminum lids (2" diameter)
- Numbers and dots (1 to 15)
- Glue
- 5 plastic lids (4" diameter)
- Numbers, dots, and pictures of items (1 to 5)

Five, Ten, Fifteen

HOW TO MAKE:

✂ Place numbers (5, 10, 15) on side of containers 1" from top.

✂ Write numbers (1 to 10) on coasters with permanent marker and place in container with 10 on outside.

✂ Attach numbers and pictures of same number of items (1, 2, 3, 4, 5) on outside of 4" plastic lids.

✂ Attach dots on inside of plastic lids the same as numbers and items on outside.

✂ Attach numbers (1 to 15) on one side and dots of same number on reverse side of aluminum lids.

STRATEGIES:

_____
_____
_____
_____
_____
_____
_____
_____

DEVELOPMENT:

_____
_____
_____
_____
_____
_____
_____

VARIATIONS:

_____
_____
_____
_____
_____
_____
_____

Color Balls

DEVELOPMENTAL LEVELS: 4–7 Years

AREAS OF DEVELOPMENT: Cognitive, Physical

BENEFITS TO CHILD: Visual discrimination; fine motor development; language development; emergent literacy

MATERIALS:

- Pizza box (15")
- 9 colored Ping-Pong balls (3 yellow, 3 pink, 3 orange)
- Mini 1¾" 12-muffin pan
- 3 plastic dishes (4" square)
- Tea diffuser (strainer)
- Hot glue gun and glue sticks
- Black permanent marker
- Cards (1" × 3")

HOW TO MAKE:

- With hot glue, attach plastic dishes inside pizza box at top.
- With hot glue, attach muffin pan below plastic dishes.
- Write color words (orange, yellow, pink) on 1" × 3" cards.
- Attach word cards to plastic dishes.
- Place balls in muffin pan.

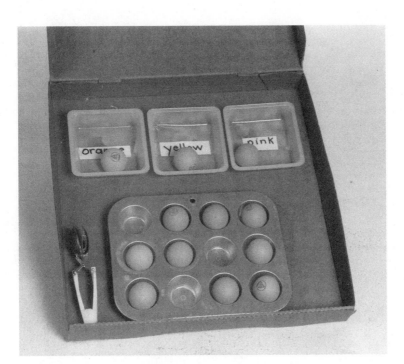

Color Balls

STRATEGIES:

_____
_____
_____
_____
_____
_____
_____
_____
_____

DEVELOPMENT:

_____
_____
_____
_____
_____
_____
_____
_____
_____
_____
_____

VARIATIONS:

_____
_____
_____
_____
_____
_____
_____
_____
_____
_____
_____

Clown Number Match

DEVELOPMENTAL LEVELS: 4–7 Years

AREAS OF DEVELOPMENT: Cognitive, Physical, Social

BENEFITS TO CHILD: Mathematics concepts; eye-hand coordination; fine motor development; cooperative play

MATERIALS:

- ⊛ Construction paper (1 red 9" × 12", 1 white 9" × 12")
- ⊛ Clear self-adhesive plastic or laminate (12" × 46")
- ⊛ Twenty 1⅞" poster board circles
- ⊛ Plastic or cloth bag for storage

HOW TO MAKE:

- ✂ Draw clowns and circles on construction paper.
- ✂ Write numbers 1 to 10 on circles on both clowns.
- ✂ Write numbers 1 to 10 on 10 poster board circles.
- ✂ Make dots to represent the numbers 1 to 10 on 10 poster board circles.
- ✂ Cover clowns and poster board circles with clear self-adhesive plastic or laminate.

Clown Number Match

STRATEGIES:

_____
_____
_____
_____
_____
_____
_____
_____
_____
_____
_____

DEVELOPMENT:

_____
_____
_____
_____
_____
_____
_____
_____
_____
_____
_____
_____

VARIATIONS:

_____
_____
_____
_____
_____
_____
_____
_____
_____
_____
_____
_____
_____

Fruit Basket

DEVELOPMENTAL LEVELS: 4–7 Years

AREAS OF DEVELOPMENT: Cognitive, Physical, Social

BENEFITS TO CHILD: Language development; emergent literacy; sensory experience; cooperative play

MATERIALS:

- Basket (to hold fruit)
- Real or artificial fruit (4 apples, 4 bananas, 2 pears, 2 lemons, 4 oranges)
- 8 library card pockets
- Sets of two pictures of each fruit (4 apples, 4 bananas, 2 pears, 2 lemons, 4 oranges) purchased or cut from magazines, catalogs, and so forth

- Clear self-adhesive plastic or laminate (8'' × 64'')
- Eight 3'' × 5'' file cards
- Black permanent marker
- Rubber cement

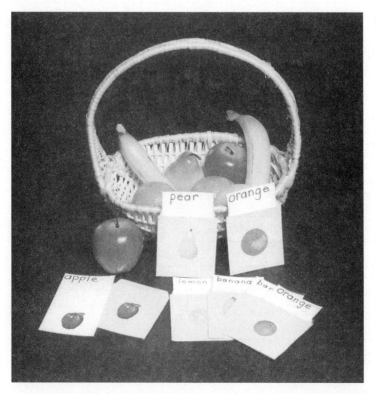

Fruit Basket

HOW TO MAKE:

- ✄ Collect fruit and place in basket.

- ✄ Write name of each piece of fruit at top of a file card.

- ✄ Attach fruit seal or picture at bottom of each word file card.

- ✄ Attach fruit seal or picture on front of a library card pocket.

- ✄ Cover all cards and card pockets with clear self-adhesive plastic or laminate.

- ✄ Cut through clear plastic so cards can be placed in library card pockets.

STRATEGIES:

_____
_____
_____
_____
_____
_____
_____
_____
_____

DEVELOPMENT:

_____
_____
_____
_____
_____
_____
_____

VARIATIONS:

_____
_____
_____
_____
_____
_____
_____
_____

Pizza Pieces

DEVELOPMENTAL LEVELS: 4–7 Years

AREAS OF DEVELOPMENT: Cognitive, Physical

BENEFITS TO CHILD: Concept development; mathematics concepts; eye-hand coordination; fine motor development; cultural awareness

MATERIALS:

- Pizza box (14" square)
- Box top pizza picture (or make a picture of pizza)
- Two 13" diameter yellow tag-board circles (or purchase pizza notepad from educational catalog)
- Black permanent marker
- Red permanent marker
- Ruler
- Rubber cement
- Clear self-adhesive plastic or laminate (14" × 56")
- Thirty-six ¾" red self-adhesive dots
- White tape

Pizza Pieces

HOW TO MAKE:

- ✀ Attach pizza picture to inside of top of pizza box with rubber cement and tape around edge of picture.
- ✀ Mark each 13" diameter yellow tagboard circle into 8 wedges of pizza.
- ✀ Color edges of each wedge with red marker to look like tomato sauce.

- ✀ Attach red dots to wedges, 1 to 8 on the 8 wedges.
- ✀ Write number words 1 to 8 in English and Spanish on the 8 pizza wedges.
- ✀ Cover all wedges with clear self-adhesive plastic or laminate.

STRATEGIES:

_____
_____
_____
_____
_____
_____

DEVELOPMENT:

_____
_____
_____
_____
_____
_____

VARIATIONS:

_____
_____
_____
_____
_____
_____
_____

Sew a Number

DEVELOPMENTAL LEVELS: 4–7 Years

AREAS OF DEVELOPMENT: Cognitive, Physical, Social

BENEFITS TO CHILD: Eye-hand coordination; letter, word, number recognition; parallel play; fine motor development

MATERIALS:

- Detergent box (7½" × 4" × 6¾")
- Black and white check self-adhesive plastic (12" × 30")
- Clear plastic self-adhesive envelope (4½" × 6½")
- Plastic canvas (twelve 4¼" diameter circles; seven 4" squares)
- Four 40" shoelaces
- Large black permanent marker
- Disinfectant solution (1 tablespoon chlorine bleach in 1 quart water)
- Poster board (3" × 6")

Sew a Number

HOW TO MAKE:

- ✄ Wash detergent box with disinfectant solution and dry thoroughly.
- ✄ Cover detergent box with black and white check self-adhesive plastic.
- ✄ Print "Sew a Number" on 3" × 6" poster board.
- ✄ Attach clear plastic self-adhesive envelope to front of box.

- ✄ Place "Sew a Number" card in envelope.
- ✄ Write numbers 1 to 20 on plastic canvas pieces.
- ✄ Store shoelaces and canvas number pieces in box.

STRATEGIES:

_____
_____
_____
_____
_____
_____
_____
_____

DEVELOPMENT:

_____
_____
_____
_____
_____
_____
_____
_____

VARIATIONS:

_____
_____
_____
_____
_____
_____
_____
_____

Animal Count

DEVELOPMENTAL LEVELS: 4–7 Years

AREAS OF DEVELOPMENT: Cognitive, Physical, Social

BENEFITS TO CHILD: Mathematics concepts; cooperative play; eye-hand coordination; language development; emergent literacy

MATERIALS:

- Specialty coffee tins with lids
  ($2\frac{3}{4}$" × $2\frac{3}{4}$" × $4\frac{1}{4}$")

- Disinfectant solution (1 tablespoon chlorine bleach in 1 quart water)

- 155 black self-adhesive dots ($\frac{3}{4}$")

- 10 pieces white paper
  (1" × $3\frac{1}{2}$")

- Black permanent marker

- Duct tape (2" × 140")

- Clear tape (2" × 140")

- Small items such as: 1 yellow rabbit, 2 white dogs, 3 green cats, 4 varied color swans, 5 white roosters, 6 varied color cows, 7 varied color ducks, 8 varied color horses, 9 varied color goats, 10 varied color sheep

Animal Count

HOW TO MAKE:

- Wash and clean coffee tins using disinfectant solution.
- Purchase or collect small items.
- Cover coffee tins with duct tape.
- Write number words 1 to 10 on 1" × 3½" cards.
- Attach word cards 1 to 10 to one wide side of each tin.
- Attach corresponding number of dots to opposite side of tins.
- Cover word cards and dots with clear tape.
- Place corresponding number of like items in each tin.

STRATEGIES:

DEVELOPMENT:

VARIATIONS:

Pizza Picnic

DEVELOPMENTAL LEVELS: 4–8 Years

AREAS OF DEVELOPMENT: Cognitive, Physical, Social

BENEFITS TO CHILD: Cooperative play; cultural; creativity; language development

MATERIALS:

- Picnic basket with handle (10" × 18" × 7")
- 4 nonbreakable plastic plates
- 4 nonbreakable plastic glasses
- 4 nonbreakable sunglasses
- Red vinyl, gingham check tablecloth (54" × 54")
- 4 red cloth napkins (12" × 12")
- Pizza (flexible, nontoxic vinyl in 7" plastic pan)
- Nonbreakable plastic spatula
- 11" × 17" tagboard, folded in middle, with words Pizza Party written on 8½" × 11" half

Pizza Picnic

HOW TO MAKE:

✂ Collect all items and place in
picnic basket.

STRATEGIES:

_____
_____
_____
_____
_____
_____
_____
_____

DEVELOPMENT:

_____
_____
_____
_____
_____
_____
_____
_____

VARIATIONS:

_____
_____
_____
_____
_____
_____
_____
_____
_____

Dinosaur Count

DEVELOPMENTAL LEVELS: 4–8 Years

AREAS OF DEVELOPMENT: Cognitive, Physical, Social

BENEFITS TO CHILD: Mathematics concepts; visual discrimination; cooperative play; fine motor development

MATERIALS:

- 5" × 3½" peel-and-stick plastic numbers (3, 4, 5, 6, 7, 8, 9)
- Clear plastic plates (9" diameter)
- 8 kinds of dinosaurs (22 blue, 12 white/green, 7 yellow, 10 brown, 12 orange/red, 3 gray/silver)
- Plastic or cloth storage bag (11" × 11")

HOW TO MAKE:

- Attach each number to a plastic plate.
- Place plates and dinosaurs in storage bag.

Dinosaur Count

STRATEGIES:

_____
_____
_____
_____
_____
_____
_____
_____
_____

DEVELOPMENT:

_____
_____
_____
_____
_____
_____
_____
_____
_____
_____

VARIATIONS:

_____
_____
_____
_____
_____
_____
_____
_____
_____
_____
_____

Count the Buttons

DEVELOPMENTAL LEVELS: 4–8 Years

AREAS OF DEVELOPMENT: Cognitive, Physical, Social

BENEFITS TO CHILD: Mathematics concepts; visual discrimination; eye-hand coordination

MATERIALS:

- 9" plastic picnic plates (2 red, 2 yellow, 2 blue)
- Sixty-three ¾" black self-stick dots
- 2" self-stick numbers (three 1s, one 2, one 3, one 5, one 6, one 8, one 9)
- 100+ assorted buttons
- Plastic or fabric storage bag

HOW TO MAKE:

- ✄ Attach numbers (3, 6, 9, 12, 15, 18) to plates.
- ✄ Attach dots to plates to match numbers.

Count the Buttons

STRATEGIES:

_____
_____
_____
_____
_____
_____
_____
_____
_____

DEVELOPMENT:

_____
_____
_____
_____
_____
_____
_____
_____
_____
_____
_____
_____

VARIATIONS:

_____
_____
_____
_____
_____
_____
_____
_____
_____
_____
_____
_____
_____

Even Number Match

DEVELOPMENTAL LEVELS: 4–8 Years

AREAS OF DEVELOPMENT: Cognitive, Physical

BENEFITS TO CHILD: Visual discrimination—words, numerals; mathematics concepts; fine motor development

MATERIALS:

- Fabric bolt
- Colored self-adhesive plastic (18" × 28")
- 6 white labels (2" × 4")
- Black large tip permanent marker
- 6 detergent lids

- 6 plastic self-stick numbers (2, 4, 6, 8, 10, 12)
- 42 craft clothespins
- Hot glue gun and glue sticks

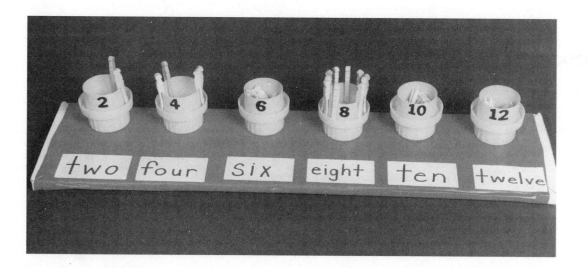

Even Number Match

HOW TO MAKE:

✂ Cover fabric bolt with colored self-adhesive plastic.

✂ Attach detergent lids along long side of fabric bolt.

✂ Attach plastic numbers (2, 4, 6, 8, 10, 12) to lids.

✂ Write number words on white labels and attach to fabric bolt below corresponding numbered lids.

STRATEGIES:

_____
_____
_____
_____
_____
_____
_____

DEVELOPMENT:

_____
_____
_____
_____
_____
_____
_____
_____

VARIATIONS:

_____
_____
_____
_____
_____
_____
_____
_____

Money Match

DEVELOPMENTAL LEVELS: 4–8 Years

AREAS OF DEVELOPMENT: Cognitive, Physical

BENEFITS TO CHILD: Mathematic concepts; value of money; relationships; problem-solving; fine motor development

MATERIALS:

- Coins (10 quarters, 10 nickels, 12 dimes, 40 pennies)

- Plastic container with lid and four sections for coin storage (e.g., dip container)

- 7 pieces construction paper (3" × 8")

- Coin strips: 5 pennies = 1 nickel; 2 nickels = 1 dime; 5 nickels = 1 quarter; 10 pennies = 1 dime; 2 dimes and 1 nickel = 1 quarter

- Clear self-adhesive plastic or laminate.

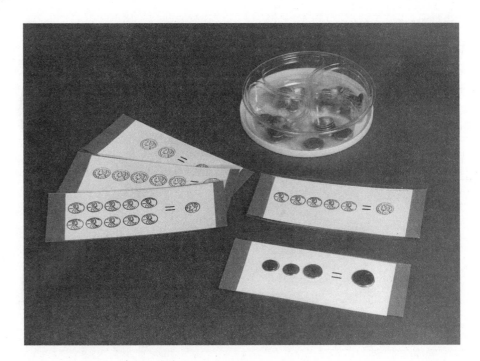

Money Match

HOW TO MAKE:

✂ Copy coins in designated sets on copy machine set at lightest color.

✂ Cut sets apart and attach to construction paper strips and cover with clear self-adhesive plastic or laminate.

STRATEGIES:

DEVELOPMENT:

VARIATIONS:

Move the Paper Clips

DEVELOPMENTAL LEVELS: 4–8 Years

AREAS OF DEVELOPMENT: Cognitive, Physical

BENEFITS TO CHILD: Sensory experience; creativity; language development

MATERIALS:

- 7½" magnet wand
- 12" diameter reel-to-reel plastic case or other round plastic container
- 150 to 200 large colored paper clips
- Hot glue gun and glue sticks

HOW TO MAKE:

- ✂ Place paper clips in case.
- ✂ Attach lid on case with hot glue and let dry for 24 hours before using.

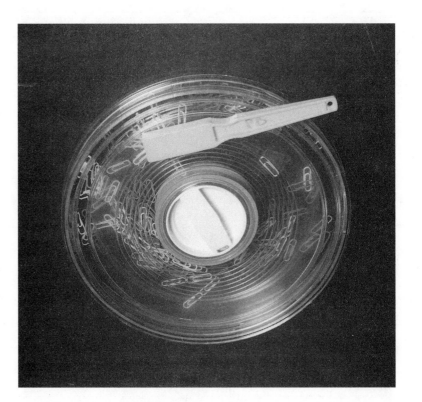

4–8 Years ✂ **273**

Move the Paper Clips

STRATEGIES:

_____
_____
_____
_____
_____
_____
_____

DEVELOPMENT:

_____
_____
_____
_____
_____
_____
_____
_____
_____
_____

VARIATIONS:

_____
_____
_____
_____
_____
_____
_____
_____
_____
_____

Spoon and Marbles

DEVELOPMENTAL LEVELS: 4–8 Years

AREAS OF DEVELOPMENT: Cognitive, Physical

BENEFITS TO CHILD: Mathematics—one-to-one correspondence; fine motor development; eye-hand coordination

MATERIALS:

- 24 marbles
- Teaspoon
- Soap dish with 24 holes
- Oval tray (6" × 8½")
- Fabric (9½" × 20½") to make 8" × 10" drawstring bag

HOW TO MAKE:

- ✂ Sew bottom and side of fabric to make bag.
- ✂ Make 1" hem at top for drawstring.
- ✂ Place teaspoon, soap dish, tray, and marbles in bag for storing.

Spoon and Marbles

STRATEGIES:

_____
_____
_____
_____
_____
_____
_____
_____
_____

DEVELOPMENT:

_____
_____
_____
_____
_____
_____
_____
_____
_____
_____
_____

VARIATIONS:

_____
_____
_____
_____
_____
_____
_____
_____
_____
_____
_____
_____

Numbers and Words

DEVELOPMENTAL LEVELS: 4–8 Years

AREAS OF DEVELOPMENT: Cognitive, Physical

BENEFITS TO CHILD: Emergent literacy; mathematics concepts; language development; eye-hand coordination; fine motor development

MATERIALS:

- 55 colored plastic animals to match number and colors written on cards
- 10 pieces poster board (7" × 8")
- Black self-adhesive numbers (1 to 10)
- Black permanent marker
- Clear self-adhesive plastic or laminate (8" × 150")

HOW TO MAKE:

- ✂ Attach numbers at top of poster board cards.
- ✂ Write on cards: one pink, two orange, three green, four yellow, five blue, six pink, seven white, eight orange, nine green, ten yellow.
- ✂ Cover front and back of cards with clear self-adhesive plastic or laminate.

Numbers and Words

STRATEGIES:

_____
_____
_____
_____
_____
_____
_____
_____
_____
_____

DEVELOPMENT:

_____
_____
_____
_____
_____
_____
_____
_____
_____
_____
_____

VARIATIONS:

_____
_____
_____
_____
_____
_____
_____
_____
_____
_____
_____
_____

Picture Tic Tac Toe

DEVELOPMENTAL LEVELS: 4–8 Years

AREAS OF DEVELOPMENT: Cognitive, Physical, Social

BENEFITS TO CHILD: Self-concept development; visual discrimination; cooperative play

MATERIALS:

- Pictures of two children—five 2½" × 3½" exactly alike pictures of each child
- Ten 2¾" × 3¾" magnetic sleeves
- Twelve 1⅜" diameter steel washers
- Hot glue gun and glue sticks
- White self-adhesive plastic tape (¾" × 60")
- Pizza box (15" square)
- Storage bag or box for pictures

Picture Tic Tac Toe

HOW TO MAKE:

✂ Place pictures in magnetic sleeves.

✂ Place white tape in pizza box to make 9 squares of approximately 4½".

✂ With hot glue attach a washer in center of each square.

STRATEGIES:

_____

_____

_____

_____

_____

_____

_____

DEVELOPMENT:

_____

_____

_____

_____

_____

_____

_____

_____

_____

_____

_____

VARIATIONS:

_____

_____

_____

_____

_____

_____

_____

_____

Key Tag

DEVELOPMENTAL LEVELS: 4–8 Years

AREAS OF DEVELOPMENT: Cognitive, Physical

BENEFITS TO CHILD: Mathematics concepts; eye-hand coordination; connect numbers and number words; fine motor skills

MATERIALS:

- Fabric bolt
- Self-adhesive plastic or laminate (18" × 28")
- 8 sticky-back plastic hooks
- 8 self-adhesive plastic numbers (1 to 8)
- 8 1½" × 3" white labels
- Black small tip permanent marker
- 36 colored key tags (6 red, 10 white, 9 yellow, 11 green)
- Small container for storing key tags

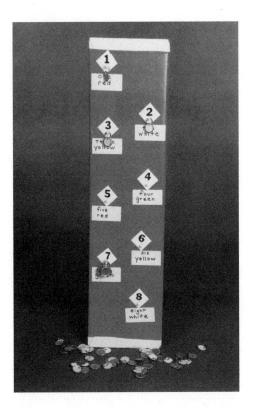

Key Tag

HOW TO MAKE:

- ✂ Cover fabric bolt with self-adhesive plastic or laminate.

- ✂ Place plastic numbers on hooks.

- ✂ Attach hooks to fabric bolt.

- ✂ Write number and color words on labels (one red, two white, three yellow, four green, five red, six yellow, seven green, eight white).

- ✂ Attach labels to fabric bolt by corresponding hooks.

STRATEGIES:

_____
_____
_____
_____
_____
_____
_____

DEVELOPMENT:

_____
_____
_____
_____
_____
_____
_____
_____
_____

VARIATIONS:

_____
_____
_____
_____
_____
_____
_____
_____
_____

Drop in the Lids

DEVELOPMENTAL LEVELS: 4–8 Years

AREAS OF DEVELOPMENT: Cognitive, Physical

BENEFITS TO CHILD: Mathematics concepts; visual discrimination—colors; eye-hand coordination; fine motor development

MATERIALS:

- Six ½-gallon milk cartons
- Red and blue self-adhesive plastic (10" × 52")
- 5" peel-and-stick plastic numbers (2, 4, 6, 8, 10, 12)
- Disinfectant (1 tablespoon chlorine bleach in 1 quart water)
- Knife
- 42 lids from gallon jugs of milk, water, juice, and so forth (2 orange, 4 yellow, 6 blue, 8 green, 10 purple, 12 black)
- Six 2" × 4" self-adhesive labels

Drop in the Lids

HOW TO MAKE:

- ✄ Wash milk cartons and lids with soapy water and disinfectant.

- ✄ Cover cartons with self-adhesive plastic, 3 red and 3 blue.

- ✄ Attach numbers to one side of milk carton.

- ✄ Write number words two, four, six, eight, ten, and twelve on self-adhesive labels.

- ✄ Attach written number words on cartons on side opposite of numbers.

- ✄ Cut ⅜" × 1¾" opening above numbers on each carton.

- ✄ Place corresponding lids in each milk carton.

STRATEGIES:

_____
_____
_____
_____
_____
_____
_____
_____

DEVELOPMENT:

_____
_____
_____
_____
_____
_____
_____
_____

VARIATIONS:

_____
_____
_____
_____
_____
_____
_____
_____

Clip the Number

DEVELOPMENTAL LEVELS: 4–8 Years

AREAS OF DEVELOPMENT: Cognitive, Physical, Social

BENEFITS TO CHILD: Mathematics concepts; cooperative play; eye-hand coordination

MATERIALS:

- Poster board (one 5" × 6", six 6" × 6", 6 ovals 6½" × 4½")
- Clear self-adhesive plastic or laminate (18" × 36")
- Detergent box (7½" × 4½" × 8½")
- Disinfectant (1 tablespoon chlorine bleach in 1 quart water)
- Large black permanent marker
- Clear plastic self-adhesive envelope (4½" × 6½")
- Red and blue colored self-adhesive plastic (30" × 8½")
- 2½" × 4½" self-adhesive numbers (1, 2, 3, 4, 5, 6)
- 2" large paper clips (28 varied colors)
- Tin container with lid for storage of paper clips

Clip the Number

HOW TO MAKE:

- Wash detergent box with disinfectant solution and dry thoroughly.
- Cover detergent box with colored self-adhesive plastic.
- Attach clear plastic self-adhesive envelope to front of detergent box.
- Write "Clip a Number" on 5" × 6" poster board card.
- Attach self-adhesive numbers to 6" × 6" poster board cards.
- Write numbers and punch corresponding number of holes on oval poster board cards.
- Cover all poster board number cards with clear self-adhesive plastic or laminate.
- Write "paper clips" on paper and attach to tin container.

STRATEGIES:

_____
_____
_____
_____
_____
_____

DEVELOPMENT:

_____
_____
_____
_____
_____
_____
_____
_____

VARIATIONS:

_____
_____
_____
_____
_____
_____

Fishing for a Number

DEVELOPMENTAL LEVELS: 4–8 Years

AREAS OF DEVELOPMENT: Cognitive, Physical, Social

BENEFITS TO CHILD: Mathematics concepts; eye-hand coordination; fine motor development; cooperative play

MATERIALS:

- ⊕ Sponge cloth (one package with two 8¼" × 8" pieces)
- ⊕ Red and black permanent markers or self-adhesive numbers 1 to 10
- ⊕ Clear self-adhesive plastic or laminate (24" × 18")
- ⊕ Poster board (12" × 18")
- ⊕ Scissors
- ⊕ ½-gallon plastic soft drink container
- ⊕ Self-adhesive cloth tape (2" × 12")
- ⊕ Tongs
- ⊕ Water

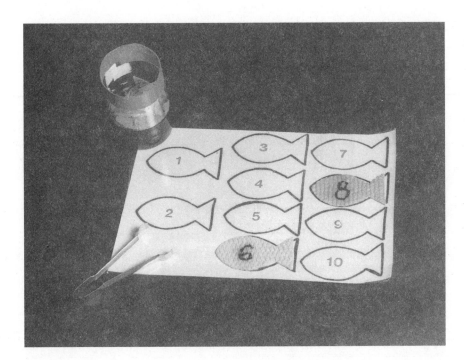

Fishing for a Number

HOW TO MAKE:

- Cut ten 4½" × 2" fish from sponge cloth.
- Write number 1 to 10 on both sides of each fish.
- Draw fish outline on poster board.
- Write number on each fish outline.
- Cover poster board with clear self-adhesive plastic or laminate.
- Cut off drink container 6" from bottom.
- Cover cut edge of container with self-adhesive cloth tape.
- Fill container ⅓ full so fish are swimming.
- Hang tongs on side of container.

STRATEGIES:

_____
_____
_____
_____
_____
_____
_____

DEVELOPMENT:

_____
_____
_____
_____
_____
_____

VARIATIONS:

_____
_____
_____
_____
_____
_____
_____

Apple Tree Two

DEVELOPMENTAL LEVELS: 4–8 Years

AREAS OF DEVELOPMENT: Cognitive, Physical, Social

BENEFITS TO CHILD: Mathematics concepts; emergent literacy; eye-hand coordination; cooperative play

MATERIALS:

- Poster board (ten 6" × 9"; ten 3" × 4" ovals)
- 1 shower curtain hook
- 1" black self-adhesive numbers (1 to 10)
- 1" varied color self-adhesive numbers (1 to 10)
- 10 library card pockets
- Varied colored dots (1 to 10) purchased or drawn on 1½" × 1¾" cards
- Black permanent marker
- Fifty-five ¾" red self-adhesive dots
- Ten 7" green trees including trunk purchased or drawn
- Clear self-adhesive plastic or laminate (9" × 150")
- Rubber cement

Apple Tree Two

HOW TO MAKE:

- ✀ Write number words at top of 6" × 9" poster board cards.
- ✀ Attach tree below number words on cards.
- ✀ Attach black numbers on tree trunk to correspond with written numbers at top of card.
- ✀ Attach red self-adhesive circles to trees to correspond with number word and number on tree trunk.
- ✀ Attach varied colored dot cards to 3" × 4" ovals.
- ✀ Attach library card pockets to back of 6" × 9" cards.
- ✀ Attach varied colored numbers to library pockets to agree with numbers on other side of card.
- ✀ Cover front and back of 6" × 9" cards and 3" × 4" ovals with clear self-adhesive plastic or laminate.
- ✀ Cut through plastic at top of library card pocket so oval card fits into pocket.

STRATEGIES:

_____
_____
_____
_____
_____
_____
_____

DEVELOPMENT:

_____
_____
_____
_____
_____
_____
_____

VARIATIONS:

_____
_____
_____
_____
_____
_____
_____

Seven, Eight, Ten

DEVELOPMENTAL LEVELS: 5–7 Years

AREAS OF DEVELOPMENT: Cognitive, Physical, Social

BENEFITS TO CHILD: Emergent literacy; visual discrimination; match colors; mathematics concepts

MATERIALS:

- 3 poster board pieces (10" × 13")
- 4½" self-adhesive numbers (7, 8, 10)
- Black permanent marker
- Clear self-adhesive plastic or laminate (13" × 60")
- Self-adhesive dots (eighteen ¾", seven 1¼")
- Colored bears (40 red, 40 blue, 40 yellow, 40 green)
- ½-gallon clear plastic container with lid for storage of bears

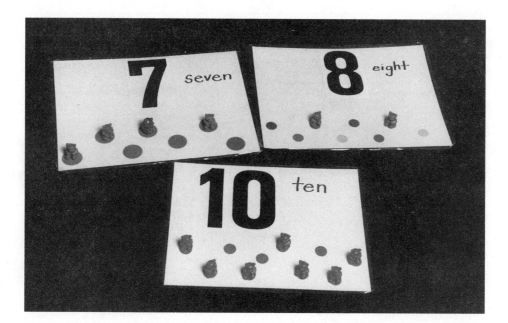

Seven, Eight, Ten

HOW TO MAKE:

✂ Place each self-adhesive number (7, 8, 10) on a 10" × 13" poster board.

✂ Write number word on right side of number.

✂ Place corresponding number of self-adhesive dots on each number card (seven 1¼" dots; eight ¾" dots, ten ¾" dots).

STRATEGIES:

_____
_____
_____
_____
_____
_____
_____
_____
_____

DEVELOPMENT:

_____
_____
_____
_____
_____
_____
_____
_____
_____
_____

VARIATIONS:

_____
_____
_____
_____
_____
_____
_____
_____
_____

Little Clothespin Match

DEVELOPMENTAL LEVELS: 5–7 Years

AREAS OF DEVELOPMENT: Cognitive, Physical

BENEFITS TO CHILD: Visual discrimination; eye-hand coordination; fine motor development

MATERIALS:

- Poster board (5" × 7")
- Permanent markers (yellow, blue, green, black)
- 1¾" clip clothespins (7 green, 5 yellow, 6 red, 6 blue)
- Clear self-adhesive plastic or laminate
- Plastic or fabric storage bag

HOW TO MAKE:

- ✂ Write color words and number of clothespins for each color along four sides of card.
- ✂ Make ⅜" color marks corresponding to each color along side of card.
- ✂ Cover card with clear self-adhesive plastic or laminate.
- ✂ Store in bag.

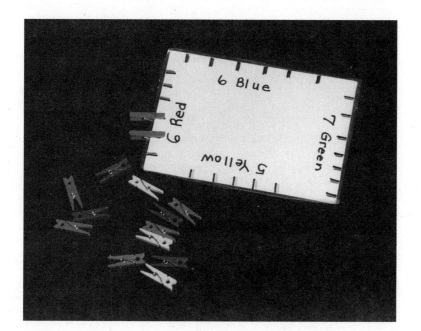

Little Clothespin Match

STRATEGIES:

_____
_____
_____
_____
_____
_____
_____
_____

DEVELOPMENT:

_____
_____
_____
_____
_____
_____
_____
_____
_____
_____

VARIATIONS:

_____
_____
_____
_____
_____
_____
_____
_____
_____
_____
_____

Add and Match

DEVELOPMENTAL LEVELS: 5–7 Years

AREAS OF DEVELOPMENT: Cognitive, Physical

BENEFITS TO CHILD: Matching—using concrete items; mathematics concepts; eye-hand coordination; relationships of number words, dots, numerals

MATERIALS:

- ⊛ Pizza box (15'')
- ⊛ 6 tongue depressors
- ⊛ 12 clip clothespins
- ⊛ Hot glue gun and glue sticks
- ⊛ Light color construction paper or tagboard (six 2'' × 3''; six 2'' × 2'')
- ⊛ Green or black fine tip permanent marker

- ⊛ 2'' plastic numbers (2, 4, 6, 8, 10, 12)
- ⊛ Different color dots for each number (2, 4, 6, 8, 10, 12)
- ⊛ Clear self-adhesive plastic or laminate

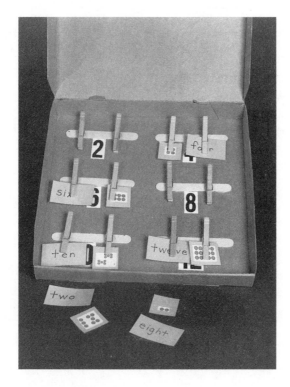

Add and Match

HOW TO MAKE:

- ✂ With hot glue, attach tongue depressors inside pizza box, 3 rows with 2 numbers in descending order from left to right and top to bottom.

- ✂ Attach plastic numbers below tongue depressors.

- ✂ With hot glue, attach two clothespins to each tongue depressor approximately 1" from each end).

- ✂ Write number words (two, four, six, eight, ten, twelve) on 2" × 3" paper or tagboard and cover with clear plastic or laminate.

- ✂ Attach dots to 2" squares of paper or tagboard and cover with clear plastic or laminate.

STRATEGIES:

DEVELOPMENT:

VARIATIONS:

Number Pyramid

DEVELOPMENTAL LEVELS: 5–8 Years

AREAS OF DEVELOPMENT: Cognitive, Physical

BENEFITS TO CHILD: Eye-hand coordination; mathematics concepts—sequencing, sorting; fine motor development; visual discrimination

MATERIALS:

- ⊕ Pizza box
- ⊕ 36 wooden ice cream spoons
- ⊕ 36 colored chenille balls (1 gray, 2 pink, 3 green, 4 yellow, 5 white, 6 brown, 7 tan, 8 red)
- ⊕ 36 thread spools
- ⊕ Permanent small tip black marker
- ⊕ Hot glue gun and glue sticks

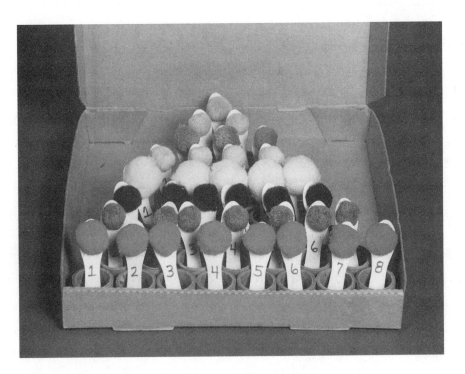

Number Pyramid

✄ With hot glue, attach thread spools in pyramid, beginning with 8 spools at bottom edge of inside of box and making each row one less ending approximately 1½'' from top).

✄ Attach chenille balls to wide end of spoons using hot glue.

✄ Write numbers in middle of each spoon (1 gray; 1, 2 pink; 1, 2, 3 green; 1, 2, 3, 4 yellow; 1, 2, 3, 4, 5 white; 1, 2, 3, 4, 5, 6 brown; 1, 2, 3, 4, 5, 6, 7 tan; 1, 2, 3, 4, 5, 6, 7, 8 red).

STRATEGIES:

_____
_____
_____
_____
_____
_____
_____

DEVELOPMENT:

_____
_____
_____
_____
_____
_____

VARIATIONS:

_____
_____
_____
_____
_____
_____

Fishing for Words

DEVELOPMENTAL LEVELS: 5–8 Years

AREAS OF DEVELOPMENT: Cognitive, Physical, Social

BENEFITS TO CHILD: Mathematics concepts; visual discrimination; emergent literacy; cooperative play

MATERIALS:

- Poster board (one 5" × 11" green; ten 1½" × 2½" white)
- Large and small black permanent markers
- Clear self-adhesive plastic or laminate
- Fish purchased or made from yellow construction paper (9" × 2")
- Fifty-five ¾" black self-adhesive dots
- 2" peel and stick numerals (1–10)

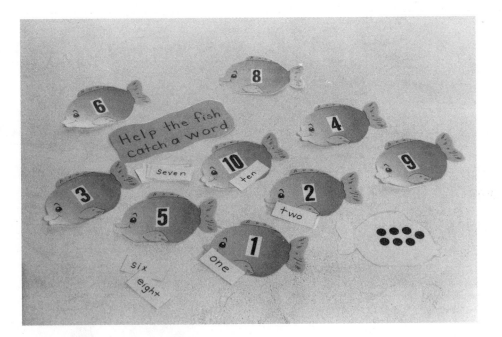

Fishing for Words

HOW TO MAKE:

- ✀ Cut out green poster board and write "Help the fish catch a word." with large marker.

- ✀ Write number words one, two, three, four, five, six, seven, eight, nine, ten on the 1½" × 2½" poster board cards.

- ✀ Attach a number (1 to 10) to each fish.

- ✀ On back of each fish, attach corresponding number of dots.

- ✀ Cover front and back of all materials with clear self-adhesive plastic or laminate.

STRATEGIES:

_____
_____
_____
_____
_____
_____
_____
_____

DEVELOPMENT:

_____
_____
_____
_____
_____
_____
_____

VARIATIONS:

_____
_____
_____
_____
_____
_____
_____
_____

Feathers

DEVELOPMENTAL LEVELS: 5–8 Years

AREAS OF DEVELOPMENT: Cognitive, Physical

BENEFITS TO CHILD: Language development; visual discrimination; fine motor development; emergent literacy; sorting

MATERIALS:

- 6 library card pockets
- 9" × 12" construction paper (red, pink, purple, green, yellow, orange)
- Black permanent marker
- Clear self-adhesive plastic or laminate (12" × 72")
- Scissors
- Plastic or fabric storage bag

Feathers

HOW TO MAKE:

- ✂ Cut feathers from construction paper (2 green, 2 yellow, 2 purple, 3 pink, 4 red, 4 orange).

- ✂ Draw feather marking with marker.

- ✂ Write feather number word and color on pocket for each color.

- ✂ Cover feathers and pockets with clear self-adhesive plastic or laminate.

- ✂ Cut slit across plastic at top of library card pocket so feathers can slip in.

STRATEGIES:

DEVELOPMENT:

VARIATIONS:

Match the Number

DEVELOPMENTAL LEVELS: 5–8 Years

AREAS OF DEVELOPMENT: Cognitive, Physical

BENEFITS TO CHILD: Mathematics concepts; eye-hand coordination; emergent literacy

MATERIALS:

- Box (9″ × 10″ × 4¾″)
- Colored self-adhesive plastic or laminate (10″ × 32″)
- 2 clear plastic self-adhesive envelopes (4″ × 6½″)
- Clear self-adhesive plastic or laminate (10″ × 108″)
- 12 library card pockets
- 24 file cards (3″ × 5″)
- Poster board (2″ × 3″; 2 yellow, 2 orange, 3 green, 1 red)
- ¾″ self-adhesive dots (10 red, 9 yellow, 6 green, 17 blue)
- White poster board (two 3″ × 6″)
- Self-adhesive numbers (2″ 1, 2, 3 green; 1″ 1, 2, 3 red and 1, 2, 3, 4 yellow)
- Numbers (1 to 12) on 1½″ × 1¾″ cards
- 1½″ × 1¾″ cards with dots (1 to 12)
- Black permanent marker
- Knife

Match the Number

HOW TO MAKE:

- ✄ Cover box with colored self-adhesive plastic or laminate.

- ✄ Cut oval 7" × 3¼" opening in top of box.

- ✄ Write numbers on 2" × 3" poster board cards (1, 2, 3 green, 1 red, 2, 3 orange, 2, 3 yellow).

- ✄ Place corresponding number of blue dots on back of each poster board card.

- ✄ Place numbers 1 to 12 on library card pockets.

- ✄ Place self-adhesive numbers and corresponding color dots on 3" × 5" file cards.

- ✄ Place dots on 3" × 5" cards and write corresponding number word (one to twelve) for each.

- ✄ Write "Match the Number" on two white 3" × 6" poster board cards.

- ✄ Cut slit through plastic on library card pocket so cards can slip in.

- ✄ Attach clear plastic self-adhesive envelopes to opposite sides of box.

- ✄ Cover front and back of all cards with clear self-adhesive plastic or laminate.

- ✄ Place all cards in box and place "Match the Number" cards in clear envelopes on box.

STRATEGIES:

_____

_____

_____

_____

_____

DEVELOPMENT:

_____

_____

_____

_____

_____

VARIATIONS:

_____

_____

_____

_____

_____

Numbers and Words
Two

DEVELOPMENTAL LEVELS: 5–8 Years

AREAS OF DEVELOPMENT: Cognitive, Physical, Social

BENEFITS TO CHILD: Mathematics concepts; observation skills; language development; fine motor development

MATERIALS:

- 5 manila envelopes (7½" × 10½")
- 5" self-adhesive numerals (2, 6, 7, 8, 9)
- Poster board (five 6" × 9", five 3" × 9", twenty 2" × 3", twenty-four 1⅞" circles)
- Black permanent marker
- Self-adhesive dots (¾"—9 red, 8 yellow, 32 black; 1⅛"—9 red)
- Clear self-adhesive plastic or laminate (12" × 240")
- 8 butterflies purchased or handmade
- Plastic or fabric bag for storage

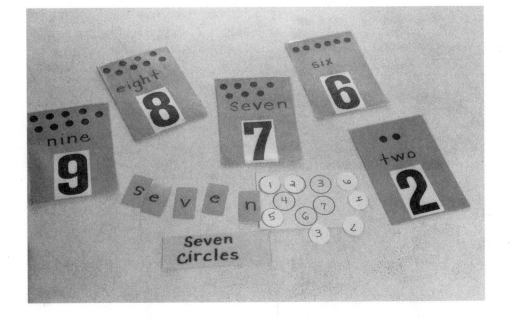

Numbers and Words Two

HOW TO MAKE:

✂ Attach a number to each envelope.

✂ Attach corresponding number of dots to each envelope.

✂ Write corresponding number word on each envelope.

✂ For envelopes, complete as follows:

2 on 6" × 9" card—outline two butterflies and write numbers 1 on one and 2 on the other; on 2" × 3" cards write two; on 3" × 9" card write two butterflies.

6 on 6" × 9" card—outline six butterflies and write 1, 2, 3, 4, 5, 6 on outlines; on 2" × 3" cards write six; on 3" × 9" card write six butterflies.

7 on 6" × 9" card—outline seven ⅞" circles and write 1, 2, 3, 4, 5, 6, 7 on outlines; on 2" × 3" cards write seven circles; on 1⅞" circles write numbers 1, 2, 3, 4, 5, 6, 7.

8 on 6" × 9" card—outline eight 1⅛" circles and color yellow; on 2" × 3" card write eight; on 3" × 9" card write eight yellow circles.

9 on 6" × 9" card—attach nine 1⅛" red dots; on 2" × 3" cards write nine; on 3" × 9" card write nine red dots; attach nine ¾" red dots to 1⅞" circles.

✂ Cover front and back of all materials with clear self-adhesive plastic or laminate.

✂ Cut through plastic so envelope flap can open.

STRATEGIES:

_____
_____
_____
_____
_____

DEVELOPMENT:

_____
_____
_____
_____
_____
_____

VARIATIONS:

_____
_____
_____
_____
_____

Marbles on a Mat

DEVELOPMENTAL LEVELS: 5–8 Years

AREAS OF DEVELOPMENT: Cognitive, Physical

BENEFITS TO CHILD: Eye-hand coordination; creativity; mathematics concepts—one-to-one correspondence; fine motor development

MATERIALS:

- Pizza box (13")
- Rubber sink mat (12" diameter with 149 holes)
- 149 marbles or beads
- Hot glue gun and glue sticks
- Plastic or fabric storage bag for marbles

HOW TO MAKE:

- Attach sink mat inside pizza box with hot glue.

Marbles on a Mat

STRATEGIES:

_____
_____
_____
_____
_____
_____
_____
_____
_____
_____

DEVELOPMENT:

_____
_____
_____
_____
_____
_____
_____
_____
_____
_____

VARIATIONS:

_____
_____
_____
_____
_____
_____
_____
_____
_____
_____

Math Recording

DEVELOPMENTAL LEVELS: 6–8 Years

AREAS OF DEVELOPMENT: Cognitive, Physical, Social

BENEFITS TO CHILD: Visual discrimination; mathematics concepts; language development; eye-hand coordination

MATERIALS:

- Detergent box (8¼" × 7¼" × 4¾")
- Blue self-adhesive plastic (8½" × 30")
- Library card envelope (3½" × 4¼")
- Clear self-adhesive plastic or laminate (4½" × 4½")
- Poster board (eight 7" × 8"; eight 3" × 6")
- Large black permanent marker
- Disinfectant solution (1 tablespoon chlorine bleach in 1 quart water)
- Ribbon (12" × 1")
- 1 pencil
- Hot glue gun and glue sticks
- White paper strips (2½" × 6½")
- Plastic container with lid (8 oz whipped topping or 1 lb margarine)
- 9 clear plastic self-adhesive envelopes (4" × 6½")

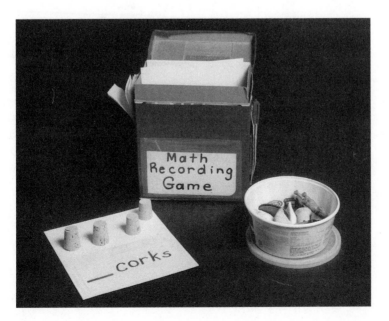

Math Recording

HOW TO MAKE:

- Wash detergent box with disinfectant and dry thoroughly.
- Cover detergent box with blue self-adhesive plastic or laminate.
- Attach 1 clear plastic self-adhesive envelope to front of detergent box.
- Use ribbon to make envelope for pencil storage and attach to one side of detergent box.
- Attach library card envelope to other side of detergent box and cover with clear self-adhesive plastic.
- Place paper strip in library card envelope.
- Attach clear plastic self-adhesive envelopes to lower part of 7" × 8" poster board pieces.
- Write words (corks, spools, keys, buttons, shells, cars, circles, animals) on 3" × 6" poster board pieces.
- Place word cards in clear envelopes on 7" × 8" poster board pieces.

STRATEGIES:

_____
_____
_____
_____
_____
_____
_____

DEVELOPMENT:

_____
_____
_____
_____
_____
_____

VARIATIONS:

_____
_____
_____
_____
_____
_____

RESOURCE INFORMATION

RECIPES

⊛ Uncooked Playdough

3 C flour	1 C salt
3 T salad oil	1 C water
Food coloring	

Mix ingredients and knead. Note: flavoring can be added for smell.

⊛ Cooked Playdough I

3 C flour	3 C water with color
3 T oil	3 T alum
1½ C salt	6 t vanilla

Mix dry ingredients. Add oil and water. Cook over medium heat, stirring constantly until thick. Remove from heat and add vanilla. Cool and store in Ziploc bag.

⊛ Cooked Playdough II

3 C flour	1½ C salt
3 C water	3 T vegetable oil
2 T cream of tartar	

Mix dry ingredients. Add water and oil. Cook over medium heat, stirring constantly until thick. Cool and store in Ziploc bag.

⊛ Fingerpaint

⅔ C corn starch	1 C cold water
3 C boiling water	1 T glycerin
1 C Ivory powder detergent or 2 T liquid Ivory	Food coloring
Oil of cloves (few drops)	

Dissolve corn starch in cold water. Smooth lumps and add to boiling water. Stir constantly. Boil until clear (not more than 1 minute). Add other ingredients. Use on paper or a washable surface for monoprints.

Homemade Paste I

        ½ C flour
        ½ C sugar
        2 C water

Mix flour and sugar. Add water and stir. Cook until thick. Place in nonbreakable container. Store in refrigerator because paste sours in one to two days at room temperature.

Homemade Past II

        ½ C flour   1 C water
        Oil of wintergreen (few drops)

Mix flour and water slowly. Boil over low heat (about 5 minutes) until thick and glossy. Cool. Add wintergreen. Store in closed nonbreakable container in refrigerator if possible.

Disinfectant

        ¼ C chlorine bleach in 1 gallon water **or**
        1 T chlorine bleach in 1 quart water

Mix daily as it loses its strength in 24 hours.

Goop

        2 boxes corn starch
        3 C water
        Food coloring to tint if desired

Mix corn starch and water in a large tub or on cafeteria trays. More corn starch or water can be added if needed. Children use fingers and hands to explore.

Scribble Crayons

        Old wax crayons
        Muffin tin

Preheat oven to 450°. Peel 5 cups of old wax crayons (break into pieces). Fill each section of a muffin tin ¾ full. Put muffin tin into oven and turn oven off. Let muffin tin sit in oven approximately 4–5 hours. Scribble crayons will pop out.

Sidewalk Chalk

        4- to 6-ounce paper cup (bathroom or kitchen size)
        ½ C Plaster of Paris
        ¼ C water
        1 t liquid or powder tempra paint (or food color)
        1 plastic spoon or popsicle stick
        Measuring cup and measuring spoon

Measure Plaster of Paris and place in paper cup. Add paint or food color. Add water and stir (should be consistency of thick paste). Set aside and let harden (approximately 20 minutes). After it has hardened, peel off the cup. Use on sidewalk (to erase chalk marks use water). (The weather may affect the amount of water needed to obtain the desired consistency of thick paste. Also, very damp or very dry weather may affect drying time.

⊛ **Rainbow Stew**

⅓ C sugar
1 C corn starch
4 C water
Red, blue, and yellow food coloring

Mix ingredients. Cook until thick. Divide into 3 bowls. Add red, blue, and yellow coloring. Then let each child pick which colors he/she would like to use in his/her bag. Tape Ziploc bag after adding about 2 tablespoons of color(s) chosen. Press air out of bag before taping. Let child push, pull, squeeze. Discuss new colors being made.

Index